D0172882

# Good Food to Go

## Healthy Lunches Your Kids Will Love

### (and actually eat)

Other books by Brenda Bradshaw

*The Baby's Table*
(with Dr. Lauren Donaldson Bramley)

*The Good Food Book for Families*
(with Dr. Cheryl Mutch)

# Good Food to Go

## Healthy Lunches Your Kids Will Love
### (and actually eat)

Brenda Bradshaw & Cheryl Mutch, M.D.

RANDOM HOUSE CANADA

PUBLISHED BY RANDOM HOUSE CANADA

Copyright © 2011 Brenda Bradshaw and Cheryl Mutch

All rights reserved under International and Pan-American Copyright Conventions. No part of this book may be reproduced in any form or by any electronic or mechanical means, including information storage and retrieval systems, without permission in writing from the publisher, except by a reviewer, who may quote brief passages in a review. Published in 2011 by Random House Canada, a division of Random House of Canada Limited, Toronto. Distributed in Canada by Random House of Canada Limited.

www.randomhouse.ca

Random House Canada and colophon are registered trademarks.

Library and Archives Canada Cataloguing in Publication

Bradshaw, Brenda (Brenda E.)
Good food to go : healthy lunches your kids will love / Brenda Bradshaw and Cheryl Mutch.

Includes index.
Issued also in electronic format.

ISBN 978-0-307-35897-4

1. Lunchbox cooking. 2. Children—Nutrition. I. Mutch, Cheryl II. Title.

TX735.B72 2011 641.5'34 C2010–907212-X

Design by Paul Dotey

Printed and bound in Canada

2 4 6 8 9 7 5 3

*To our children, Charlie, Chelsea, Ashley and Elliotte,*
*and to our mothers, Val and Janet*

# TABLE OF CONTENTS

Foreword

In the 20 years that I have been practising pediatrics, many of the most frequent questions raised by parents revolve around their children's nutrition and eating habits. As I reflect on my own family, nutrition is something my wife and I discuss with regards to our children—and we don't always agree! The issue of school lunches is a frequent source of debate in our home. The media is full of advice and dire warnings about what you should and should not be giving your children, but this advice is often based on current fashion more than good evidence or sense.

With the great progress and advances of the last 50 years, family life and schedules seem to have become more rushed and hectic. So many choices are available for children, and school and extra-curricular programs fill the day while parents battle to find the time to cook and prepare meals. Families are bombarded with easy fast food options and accessibility on every corner—and sometimes even in the school itself. Children today have an increasingly sedentary lifestyle as they spend more and more time in front of a screen and less time playing outside. This situation is compounded by increasing exposure to unhealthy food choices, which has contributed to a tripling of the rate of obesity in children over the last 30 years in North America. We are starting to see a rise in the appearance of diseases that were previously restricted to adults in younger and younger children. We need to start thinking more carefully about what we are feeding our children, and what they are munching on at school is a good place to start. In order to do the right thing, we need some practical, affordable and easy strategies for packing nutritious lunches within the confines of our already busy schedules and tight budgets. We also need a bit of information about what is going on in our children developmentally and how to use this knowledge to help get them interested and invested in making good food choices.

There are many things that I like about this book. It is full of practical and nutritionally sound advice. In a straightforward fashion the authors share many pearls regarding the what, the how and the why of "good food" and, specifically, healthy lunches. They share some great strategies for making feeding your children fun, healthy and a lot easier. The book is organized in a reader-friendly manner, making it easy to find what you're looking for and providing so many ideas and options in each category. The recipes look appetizing, easy to prepare and nutritious. The lists and resources are helpful and well researched. The authors bring their years of training and experience in nutrition and pediatrics to the reader in excellent, scientifically sound "bite-size" pieces.

The household I grew up in must have been similar to that of the late American comedian Buddy Hackett, who said, "As a child my family's menu consisted of two choices: take it or leave it." Let's hope that times have changed for the better—and so should lunches.

I have a feeling that this book is going to become an invaluable resource for parents for years to come!

Jeremy Friedman, MB. ChB, FRCP(C), FAAP
Head, Division of Pediatric Medicine,
The Hospital for Sick Children, Toronto
Author of *Canada's Baby Care Book* and
*Canada's Toddler Care Book*

# Introduction

If you are like many parents, the thought of packing healthy, homemade lunches day in and day out fills you with dread. With increasing awareness of the need for healthy, balanced meals, this task becomes even more important. Your child's lunch should meet the recommendations of Canada's Food Guide. Yet it also needs to be hot enough, cold enough or crisp enough to withstand a morning in the cloakroom. The lunch should be safely packaged and in environmentally friendly containers.

And with peanut allergies on the rise many schools are now nut free, eliminating a favourite and easy standby: peanut butter.

Obviously, you want your child's lunch to be homemade and healthy but your time is limited. More importantly, the lunch needs to be kid friendly and delicious because, after all, the healthiest lunch isn't very healthy if it goes uneaten.

Take heart. You are already on the road to creating healthy, environmentally friendly lunches that your children will devour. *Good Food to Go* fuses the how-to's of creating wholesome, homemade lunches with the latest information on food and nutrition. Our practical tips will help you make environmentally conscious food choices and eliminate lunch-box waste. This will help your family eat for a healthier future.

Instead of making an "old-school" sandwich, try our pita pockets, wraps, bagels and picnic style lunches. On winter days hot meals will warm hungry tummies, and homemade baked goods will have your kids grinning from ear to ear. Turn favourite dinners into delicious leftovers for tomorrow's lunch. Alongside the easy-to-prepare recipes, we will provide you with the latest nutritional information to ensure your kids are getting what they need to thrive.

As working parents ourselves, we understand how busy life can be. We offer advice on how to involve your kids in preparing food and packing lunch boxes, ultimately freeing up your valuable time. Many of our recipes outline what can be done the night before, while others can be made in bulk and frozen, facilitating easy, last-minute lunches. Our meal planners will guide you through the week, providing your kids with a healthy variety of tasty and nutritious lunches.

Given that children consume approximately $1/3$ of their daily calories at school, what goes into your children's lunch boxes is vital to their well-being. Eating a healthy lunch will improve their attention span, behaviour and learning ability. They will experience less fatigue and will have more energy to work and play. Furthermore, healthy eating provides the building blocks for growth and development and reduces the possibility of developing nutrition-related diseases. Congratulations—you and your children are on the road to a healthy and happy school year!

I.

Getting
Started

## Educate to Motivate

No matter how beautifully packaged and healthy your child's lunch may be, if it comes home uneaten or, worse yet, winds up in the garbage, all your hard work is wasted. Research tells us that children who are involved in preparing their food are more likely to eat it. Therefore, it's important to get your kids involved from the outset. After all, we know kids won't eat what they don't like, especially if you are not there.

Kids of all ages can take part in preparing and choosing the foods that go into their lunches. Young children can wash vegetables and fruit, help with baking and mix sandwich spreads. With guidance, older children can make sandwiches and cut fruits and vegetables, while high school students can independently pack their own lunches. However, it is important to understand that things don't always go as smoothly as planned. If you are unhappy with the type of lunches that your teen packs, consider getting him to clean up the kitchen after dinner while you start the lunch. Preparing food for someone else is an act of generosity and nurturing. Spend a few extra minutes together packing leftovers and choosing which fruits and snacks to include.

Co-operative meal planning is a wonderful opportunity to teach your children about the importance of healthy eating. Turn to the copy of Canada's Food Guide starting on page 11. Remind your kids of the 4 food groups and explain how each group provides our bodies with a different set of key nutrients. For example, Vegetables and Fruit help us stay healthy by providing us with important vitamins, minerals, fibre and antioxidants.

Meat and Alternatives provide us with energy, iron and protein. Energy gives us the power needed to accomplish our daily tasks: working, playing, growing and learning. Protein helps us stay alert and provides our bodies with the tools needed to build and repair body tissue. When Brenda's son, Charlie, was young, he was reluctant to eat chicken sandwiches until she explained that chicken is packed full of protein, the nutrient needed to build strong muscles. To this day, Charlie's favourite lunch is the Chicken Souvlaki Wrap (page 74).

Milk and Alternatives supply us with protein, vitamin D and calcium. Calcium and vitamin D are the nutrients needed to build healthy bones and strong teeth. Building a skeleton without vitamin D and calcium is like building a sandcastle without sand.

Finally, Grain Products provide us with carbohydrates and fibre. Carbohydrates give us energy and supply our brain with the fuel it needs to think and learn. Fibre keeps our bowels working regularly and its intake is associated with reduced risk of various diseases including heart disease, diabetes and obesity.

## Canada's Food Guide

Canada's Food Guide is designed to help Canadians establish a healthy pattern of eating that meets their nutritional requirements, while lessening the possibility of developing chronic diseases. It does so by recommending the amounts and types of foods Canadians should eat.

Source: Canada's Food Guide. Health Canada.
Reproduced with the permission of the Ministry of Health, 2007.

# Recommended Number of *Food Guide Servings* per Day

| | Children | | | Teens | | Adults | | | |
|---|---|---|---|---|---|---|---|---|---|
| Age in Years | 2-3 | 4-8 | 9-13 | 14-18 | | 19-50 | | 51+ | |
| Sex | Girls and Boys | | | Females | Males | Females | Males | Females | Males |
| **Vegetables and Fruit** | 4 | 5 | 6 | 7 | 8 | 7-8 | 8-10 | 7 | 7 |
| **Grain Products** | 3 | 4 | 6 | 6 | 7 | 6-7 | 8 | 6 | 7 |
| **Milk and Alternatives** | 2 | 2 | 3-4 | 3-4 | 3-4 | 2 | 2 | 3 | 3 |
| **Meat and Alternatives** | 1 | 1 | 1-2 | 2 | 3 | 2 | 3 | 2 | 3 |

The chart above shows how many Food Guide Servings you need from each of the four food groups every day.

Having the amount and type of food recommended and following the tips in *Canada's Food Guide* will help:

• Meet your needs for vitamins, minerals and other nutrients.
• Reduce your risk of obesity, type 2 diabetes, heart disease, certain types of cancer and osteoporosis.
• Contribute to your overall health and vitality.

## What is One Food Guide Serving?
**Look at the examples below.**

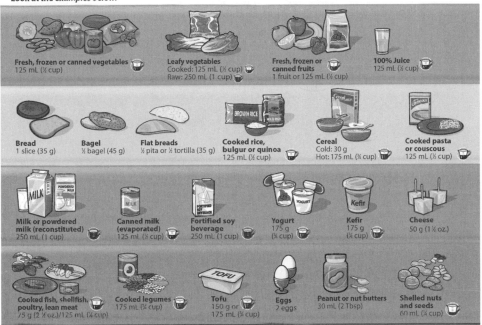

**Fresh, frozen or canned vegetables**
125 mL (½ cup)

**Leafy vegetables**
Cooked: 125 mL (½ cup)
Raw: 250 mL (1 cup)

**Fresh, frozen or canned fruits**
1 fruit or 125 mL (½ cup)

**100% Juice**
125 mL (½ cup)

**Bread**
1 slice (35 g)

**Bagel**
½ bagel (45 g)

**Flat breads**
½ pita or ½ tortilla (35 g)

**Cooked rice, bulgur or quinoa**
125 mL (½ cup)

**Cereal**
Cold: 30 g
Hot: 175 mL (¾ cup)

**Cooked pasta or couscous**
125 mL (½ cup)

**Milk or powdered milk (reconstituted)**
250 mL (1 cup)

**Canned milk (evaporated)**
125 mL (½ cup)

**Fortified soy beverage**
250 mL (1 cup)

**Yogurt**
175 g
(¾ cup)

**Kefir**
175 g
(¾ cup)

**Cheese**
50 g (1 ½ oz.)

**Cooked fish, shellfish, poultry, lean meat**
75 g (2 ½ oz.)/125 mL (½ cup)

**Cooked legumes**
175 mL (¾ cup)

**Tofu**
150 g or
175 mL (¾ cup)

**Eggs**
2 eggs

**Peanut or nut butters**
30 mL (2 Tbsp)

**Shelled nuts and seeds**
60 mL (¼ cup)

### Oils and Fats

- Include a small amount – 30 to 45 mL (2 to 3 Tbsp) – of unsaturated fat each day. This includes oil used for cooking, salad dressings, margarine and mayonnaise.
- Use vegetable oils such as canola, olive and soybean.
- Choose soft margarines that are low in saturated and trans fats.
- Limit butter, hard margarine, lard and shortening.

13

## *Make each Food Guide Serving count...*
### *wherever you are – at home, at school, at work or when eating out!*

▸ **Eat at least one dark green and one orange vegetable each day.**
- Go for dark green vegetables such as broccoli, romaine lettuce and spinach.
- Go for orange vegetables such as carrots, sweet potatoes and winter squash.

▸ **Choose vegetables and fruit prepared with little or no added fat, sugar or salt.**
- Enjoy vegetables steamed, baked or stir-fried instead of deep-fried.

▸ **Have vegetables and fruit more often than juice.**

▸ **Make at least half of your grain products whole grain each day.**
- Eat a variety of whole grains such as barley, brown rice, oats, quinoa and wild rice.
- Enjoy whole grain breads, oatmeal or whole wheat pasta.

▸ **Choose grain products that are lower in fat, sugar or salt.**
- Compare the Nutrition Facts table on labels to make wise choices.
- Enjoy the true taste of grain products. When adding sauces or spreads, use small amounts.

▸ **Drink skim, 1%, or 2% milk each day.**
- Have 500 mL (2 cups) of milk every day for adequate vitamin D.
- Drink fortified soy beverages if you do not drink milk.

▸ **Select lower fat milk alternatives.**
- Compare the Nutrition Facts table on yogurts or cheeses to make wise choices.

▸ **Have meat alternatives such as beans, lentils and tofu often.**

▸ **Eat at least two Food Guide Servings of fish each week.***
- Choose fish such as char, herring, mackerel, salmon, sardines and trout.

▸ **Select lean meat and alternatives prepared with little or no added fat or salt.**
- Trim the visible fat from meats. Remove the skin on poultry.
- Use cooking methods such as roasting, baking or poaching that require little or no added fat.
- If you eat luncheon meats, sausages or prepackaged meats, choose those lower in salt (sodium) and fat.

*Enjoy a variety of foods from the four food groups.*

*Satisfy your thirst with water!*

Drink water regularly. It's a calorie-free way to quench your thirst. Drink more water in hot weather or when you are very active.

* Health Canada provides advice for limiting exposure to mercury from certain types of fish. Refer to www.healthcanada.gc.ca for the latest information.

Ideally, a healthy lunch box includes foods from all 4 food groups. Given the daily number of servings required from both Grain Products and Vegetables and Fruit, it makes sense to include at least 2 servings from each of these groups. This may seem like a lot, but bear in mind serving sizes are small. A sandwich made with 2 slices of whole wheat bread or a whole wheat bagel is equivalent to 2 servings of Grain Products. A lunch containing 2 broccoli florets and an apple counts as 2 servings of Vegetables and Fruit. Adding vegetables to sandwiches is a great way to add an extra serving of veggies to your child's diet.

## Get the Kids Involved

Sit down with your children and brainstorm lists of foods that they like from each of the food groups. Use these lists to compile a number of lunches that incorporate all the food groups. For more lunch box ideas go through this book with your children and pick out a number of recipes to try. Our Meal Planners, found in Appendix 1, give examples of healthy lunches that include all 4 food groups.

### Think Outside the Lunch Box

Resist the temptation to send your child to school with the same old sandwich, day in and day out. A healthy diet is a varied one. This is because each of the food groups offers a different set of key nutrients, while different foods within each group also provide different nutrients. For example, both salmon and beef contain iron and protein, with beef containing significantly more iron, while salmon is an excellent source of omega-3 fatty acids.

Creating variety in your children's lunch boxes also means ensuring they are eating foods with different tastes and textures. Consider alternating between soups (Chapter 5), leftovers (Chapter 7), picnic style lunches (Chapter 4), salads (Chapter 6) and sandwiches (Chapter 3). Even children with limited palates have their favourites, and it just makes sense to rotate them throughout the week.

Getting Started

Once you have come up with a number of lunch box ideas, put the list on the refrigerator and encourage your children to add a few more foods or recipes to the list every so often. From this list, plan out a week's worth of lunches. This may seem time-consuming, but we know that those who plan their meals in advance have a tendency to eat a healthier diet.

Take your children grocery shopping and occasionally take the opportunity to talk to them about resisting the "kid appeal" of cleverly packaged, processed foods. Young children may make food choices based on what they see their friends eating or what they see on TV. Explain the difference between highly processed foods and whole foods. Highly processed foods tend to be higher in salt, fat, sugar and chemical additives while providing minimal nutritional value. Although it is OK to eat these foods on occasion, eating them daily can cause our bodies to feel slow and sluggish and may lead to excess weight gain.

The easiest way to avoid the appeal of processed and packaged foods is to stick to the outer aisles of the grocery store. If you find your child veering toward the snack aisle, distract her by involving her in the decision-making process. "Should we buy apples or pears today?" Make a point of spending some time in the produce section. Ask her to choose the fruits and vegetables she likes, while encouraging her to pick out some new ones to try. You may be surprised how willing she is to experiment when she makes her own choices.

Eating habits are learned behaviours. Those who are taught healthy habits early are more likely to sustain them throughout their lives. Children who are taught what constitutes a healthy lunch will know how to make one when the time comes. You can help them do this by organizing your refrigerator and pantry so that all the food groups are represented and easily accessible. Use the following chart to help you organize your kitchen.

## Organizing Your Kitchen

In the refrigerator you could have:

Milk and Alternatives: yogurt, tzatziki and other dips for veggies, lower fat milk (2%, 1% or skim) or fortified soymilk, light cream cheese and a variety of lower fat cheeses

Meat and Alternatives: precooked meats ready to go for sandwiches, tofu, eggs, hard-boiled eggs ready to go for the lunch box, peanut butter, as well as other nut and seed butters, hummus and other bean dips

Vegetables and Fruit: a large selection of washed fruit and veggies ready to go for sandwiches, salads and snacks. Have a melon, papaya, pineapple or other fruit cut up and ready to eat. When berries are in season, have a selection of washed berries ready for eating.

In the freezer you could have:

Vegetables and Fruit: a variety of frozen fruit and vegetables, as well as homemade vegetable soups

Grain Products: a variety of whole grain breads, wraps, bagels and pita pockets to be used to make sandwiches. Extra homemade baked goods and muffins can also be stored in the freezer.

In the pantry you could have:

Meat and Alternatives: a variety of nuts, seeds, dried legumes, canned tuna, canned salmon, canned baked beans and legumes

Grain Products: a variety of whole grain cereals and crackers, air-popped popcorn, pasta, a variety of whole grains (quinoa, bulgur, whole grain and wild rice) and your own homemade baked goods

Vegetables and Fruit: canned corn, canned tomatoes, tomato paste, canned fruit packed in juice, a selection of dried fruit and a bowl of washed fruit sitting on your counter ready to go.

# Developing a Positive Lunch Box Rapport

You can control what goes into your child's lunch box but not necessarily what goes into your child. Developing a positive lunch box rapport is one of the keys to improving your child's nutritional intake. Encourage children to bring their leftovers home. As frustrating as it may be to see an uneaten sandwich or apple, keep your comments to yourself. If you harp on it, the uneaten food will likely end up in the garbage and you will be none the wiser.

Knowledge is power. Find out why the lunch is not being eaten. Perhaps there was too much mustard on the sandwich or the tomato made it soggy. If this is the case, simply make the changes and try again.

Find out what it is about other children's lunches that appeal to your kids. If your daughter is envious of the convenience foods, see if you can offer her some healthier alternatives. Instead of potato chips, try air-popped popcorn or homemade bits and bites (page 94). For the occasional treat, there is no harm in a small portion of chips, but opt for baked instead of fried. If packaged cookies or doughnuts appeal, try our homemade cookies, granola bars and healthy muffins (Chapter 8). Your homemade baked goods are almost certainly more nutritious than typical store-bought alternatives.

Many children complain about not having enough time to eat their lunches, but often it's a matter of conflicting agendas. What 7-year-old boy will take the time to peel an orange when he can be outside playing? For many children, lunch is simply a refuelling stop, and if it takes too long to eat something, they simply won't. For these kids, "picnic style" lunches composed of ready-to-go, bite-sized morsels of food often work best. Be sure to pack portable snacks, such as an apple or a homemade granola bar, that can be eaten on the go. For more information on picnic style lunches, see Chapter 4.

Children who skip their lunches are often famished when they come home. If this is the case and the leftover food is still fresh, there is no reason why it cannot be eaten after school. However it's imperative that you never force your child to eat an unfinished lunch. This tactic will likely backfire, ensuring that future leftovers end up in the garbage or, even worse, at the bottom of a locker for months! Furthermore, research tells us that children who are forced or pressured to eat have a tendency to eat less.

## What Should My Children Be Drinking at School?

At school, children should drink milk, water or 100% pure fruit or vegetable juice. Canada's Food Guide recommends that all Canadians over the age of 2 drink 2 cups of milk or fortified soy beverage every day in order to get adequate vitamin D and calcium. However, we know that ⅓ of Canadian children do not get the recommended number of servings of milk products per day.[1] Packing milk with lunch is an easy way to improve your child's odds of meeting this requirement. Milk can be kept cool in a pre-chilled Thermos. (To chill the Thermos, fill it with ice water and let it stand for 5 minutes.) If your child is a reluctant milk drinker, don't be afraid to flavour it with a little chocolate syrup if this is how he likes it. It is better for your child to drink chocolate milk than no milk at all. Over time you can slowly decrease the amount of syrup you add to the milk.

### Juice Abuse

Packing 100% pure fruit or vegetable juice in the lunch box is one way to get a serving of Vegetables and Fruit into your child. However, in the case of juice, it is very easy to overdo it. Children have a tendency to favour sweet foods; preferring apple juice over an apple. And, although the juice contains some vitamin C and minerals, it lacks the fibre found in the whole fruit. Furthermore, children who drink excessive amounts of juice have a tendency to lose their appetite and miss out on important nutrients found in whole foods. Excessive juice drinking can lead to diarrhea and dental cavities. Young juice drinkers tend to turn from juice to soda pop as they get older.

If you are serving juice, always choose 100% pure fruit and/or vegetable juice and limit it to no more than once a day. According to Canada's Food Guide, half a cup of juice is equivalent to 1 serving. If you serve juice with breakfast, pack milk or water for lunch. Keep soda pop, fruit drinks, fruit cocktails and punches out of the lunch box. Loaded with sugar, these drinks contain little or no real fruit juice.

The advantage of packing juice and water in a stainless steel water bottle is that it can be refilled with water throughout the day. It is especially important that children drink lots of water on hot days or after physical activity. This is because children are more susceptible than adults to dehydration, which can lead to fatigue, loss of concentration and dizziness. Water is always the best thirst quencher. It adds zero calories to the diet and has little impact on appetite.

### Nix the Energy Drinks!

Avoid offering so-called "energy drinks" to your kids. These beverages, loaded with sugar or artificial sweeteners, are designed for extreme athletes and often contain high amounts of sodium, caffeine and other unwanted chemical additives. In fact, some of these drinks contain as much as 10 times the amount of caffeine found in a single can of cola.[2] It has long been known that the consumption of caffeine has a negative impact on sleep and can cause hyperactivity in sensitive children. In fact, poor sleep quality and quantity during adolescence has been associated with mood disorders, exacerbation of asthma, obesity, lower sense of well-being and poor school performance.[3]

## Avoiding the Morning Rush

Mornings are hectic times for most families. The best way to avoid the morning rush is to prepare as much as you can the night before. Set out the lunch box and any containers and utensils you may need. Organize the ingredients and wash the fruit and vegetables, many of which can be packaged and stored in the refrigerator overnight. Sandwich spreads can be mixed and many of the salads can be prepacked. To save precious morning minutes, numerous recipes in this book outline what can be done the night before.

Use the weekends to make baked goods and homemade soups. In the same amount of time, you can double or even triple recipes. Ask your child what his favourite dinner is and plan for leftovers. Prepare extra pasta, chili, salad, soup, vegetables and rice. Many leftovers can be frozen in individual containers for later use. Instead of relying on processed meats, which tend to be high in fat, sodium and chemical additives, cook extra meat at dinner to be used in sandwiches. For more information on leftovers, see Chapter 7: Encore Performances.

## Avoiding the Lunch Box Landfill

The typical school-aged child packing an old-fashioned "brown bag" lunch creates, on average, an astounding 67 pounds of waste per year. The use of foil, plastic wrap, sandwich bags and single-use packaged items such as granola bars, chips, yogurt, drink cans, cartons and boxes have become the norm. Admittedly these products are convenient, but they come with a long-term cost. Much of this waste ultimately ends up in landfills or incinerators that pump toxic chemicals into our atmosphere.

Instead of brown-bagging it, we would like to motivate you to create litterless lunches. It's a wonderful way to inspire your children to make environmentally conscious decisions, as well as help them understand how their actions can have a positive impact on the world around them. A waste-free lunch contains no packaging so there is nothing to throw away other than the odd bits of biodegradable waste: banana peels, cherry pits, apple cores, etc., which can all be composted. After all, the best way to reduce garbage is not to create it in the first place.

In addition to minimizing your environmental footprint, waste-free lunches have other advantages. They tend to be healthier and more economical. It is less expensive to buy in bulk. Instead of buying a plastic-wrapped package of 5 individual juice boxes, buy 100% pure fruit juice in bulk and pour it into a stainless steel water bottle. Rather than buying single-serving yogurt containers, buy a large container and make your own yogurt pots (page 86). Furthermore, many of the processed lunch box products that are individually packaged and marketed for children tend to be high in salt, sugar, fats and unwanted chemical additives. Talking to your kids about the environmental impact of packaged foods will help them realize how "uncool" these products really are.

## The Juice Box Dilemma

A juice box or Tetra Pak is an aseptic container. This means that it is manufactured and filled under sterile conditions and therefore requires no refrigeration or preservatives to remain germ free. They are typically made from 6 layers of paper, plastic and foil that are bonded together. The problem with juice boxes, like that of many single-use drink containers, is that ultimately many of them end up in landfills and, because of their laminated construction, juice boxes are one of the most inorganic items around, retaining their weight and volume for many years to come.

The manufacturers of aseptic containers say they are environmentally friendly. They argue that they take up less room on trucks and require no refrigeration, which ultimately means they use less energy during transportation. Many communities in Canada recycle aseptic containers as part of their municipal recycling program. Juice boxes can also be returned to local recycling depots or to the place of purchase for a deposit refund, and many schools now have juice box recycling programs.

While recycling the Tetra Pak is possible, the fact remains that most North American recycling plants are not equipped for hydropulping, the process needed to recycle aseptic containers. At present the vast majority of recycled Canadian juice boxes are processed in Asia. Just imagine the fuel required to ship and recycle single-use juice boxes around the world.

So consider buying juice in bulk. By packing your child's drink in a reusable bottle, you are creating less waste, regardless of whether it ends up being recycled or, even worse, in a landfill. It's just common sense.

# The Equipment

Ideally, your child's lunch box should be large enough to accommodate a Thermos, several reusable containers and a stainless steel water bottle. Over the course of the school year, you will need a number of reusable stainless steel or plastic containers. These containers should be stackable and of varying sizes to accommodate a variety of menu options. If buying plastic containers, choose ones that are bisphenol A free and dishwasher safe. Lids need to be leak-proof but accessible so that young children can open them with ease. Purchase a wide-mouth, stainless steel Thermos. These Thermoses tend to be vacuum insulated, making them more durable than traditional glass Thermoses. Instead of using paper napkins and plastic cutlery, opt for cloth napkins and metal cutlery.

Rather than buying a typical North American lunch box, you can always opt for a "bento style" lunch box. Increasingly popular, bento boxes are modelled after traditional Japanese lunch boxes. A typical bento box consists of a number of sealable compartments within a single lunch box. To learn more about or to purchase a bento style lunch box go to www.laptoplunches.com.

And don't forget to label everything so that misplaced items have a better chance of finding their way home!

## Bisphenol A

Developed over 100 years ago, bisphenol A (BPA) is an industrial chemical used to make polycarbonate, a clear hard plastic. Polycarbonate is used in the production of many household products, including plastic drinking bottles and food containers. It is also found in epoxy resins, which are commonly used to line metal drink and food cans. BPA levels were measured in Canadians for the first time between 2007 and 2009. BPA was found in 91 per cent of urine samples tested. The levels in children were found to be higher than in adults, with levels in teenagers being the highest of all.[4]

Since the 1930s, BPA has been known to be an endocrine disruptor.

This means it can mimic natural hormones in the body. Early childhood development appears to be the period of greatest sensitivity to the effects of BPA. Studies indicate that low levels of BPA can affect the development of the nervous system and subsequent behaviour in lab animals. Further animal studies indicate that BPA may be linked to obesity,[5] prostate cancer,[6] breast cancer,[7] and declining fertility rates.[8] While these studies are very concerning, we do not have a definitive understanding of how these findings relate to human health.

In 2008, Canada, concerned for the safety of young children and infants, became the first country to take steps to ban the sale of polycarbonate baby bottles, while continuing to study the effects of BPA on human health.

The government reassures the population that canned foods are safe and can continue to be part of a balanced diet.[9] Regardless, it makes good sense to minimize your family's exposure. One of the best ways to do this is to eat fresh and dried foods more often and look for BPA-free canned goods, which are beginning to appear on supermarket shelves. Any of the recipes in this book that call for legumes can be made with either dried or canned beans. The cooking instructions for dried beans can be found on page 105.

When purchasing food and beverages in containers, look for those that are BPA free. Many manufacturers clearly state that their products are BPA free, but if you are unsure, contact the manufacturer. And remember, whether or not your plastic containers are microwave safe, it makes good sense to avoid heating foods in plastic or pouring hot liquids into plastic containers. This is because heat promotes the leaching of chemicals, while cold inhibits it. So while it is considered safe to freeze foods in plastic containers, you don't want to be heating foods in them.

## Lunch Box Safety

School lunches generally sit in the cloakroom or locker all morning long. Prolonged exposure to room temperature increases the risk of bacterial growth and contamination. The easiest way to reduce this risk is to pack your child's lunch in a thermally insulated lunch box with an ice pack. Ice packs are designed to keep food cold for 4 to 6 hours. Or, to save space, freeze your child's water bottle or yogurt. By lunchtime the drink or yogurt should be thawed. As a general rule, foods that come out of the refrigerator need to be kept cold. This includes dairy products, eggs, meat and mayonnaise, which should be packed next to the ice pack.

The best way to keep hot foods hot is to preheat your child's Thermos by pouring boiling water in it and letting it stand for 5 minutes. To keep cold foods cold, pour ice water into the Thermos and let it stand for 5 minutes. Lunch boxes should be cleaned daily with hot soapy water and wiped out once a week with a diluted bleach solution.

## The Obesity Epidemic

Obesity is the most common nutrition-related problem in North America, with rates in children that have almost tripled in the last 25 years. Approximately 26 per cent of Canadian children ages 2 to 17 are currently overweight or obese.[10] Physical complications of obesity include type 2 diabetes, high blood pressure, elevated cholesterol, liver disease, bone and joint problems, respiratory problems (including asthma), sleep disorders and fatigue. Furthermore, overweight children are more at risk for psychological problems such as depression, anxiety and low self-esteem.

Although there is a genetic component to obesity, the rate of increase points to environmental factors. Simply put, childhood has changed. Our children spend less active time playing outside than they used to. Instead they spend much of their free time inside, pursuing sedentary activities such as watching TV, playing computer games and/or texting friends. More children are being driven between home and school and after-school activities instead of walking or riding their bikes as past generations did. We know that over half of Canadian children are not active enough for healthy growth and development.[11]

## Did You Know that Your Child's Weight May Influence the Onset of Puberty?

Fat cells produce estrogen, the female sex hormone. Because overweight girls have more estrogen in their bodies, they tend to experience an earlier onset of puberty. For boys, this increase in estrogen counteracts the testosterone, causing a delay in puberty.

Our eating habits have also changed. Children are consuming more processed foods and high-calorie beverages, including soda pop, sports drinks, fruit cocktails and even expensive coffee-based beverages. We are dining out and frequenting fast food restaurants more than ever before, and portion sizes continue to increase. As a result, today's children are consuming many more high calorie foods, while not getting enough exercise to burn off the added calories.

## Lean Lunch Box Tips

- Keep highly processed and packaged foods out of the lunch box.
- Limit products made with refined flour like white bread, cookies, cakes, doughnuts, etc.
- Pack water or skim milk to drink.
- Pack fruit and vegetables for snacks.
- Choose lower fat dairy products.
- Avoid using butter in sandwiches and use lower fat condiments, such as low-fat mayonnaise, mustard, tzatziki and hummus.
- Pack higher fibre foods such as whole grain products, beans, lentils, fruits and vegetables. These foods are filling and tend to be relatively low in calories.
- Pack salads with oil- and vinegar-based dressings and avoid high calorie add-ons such as bacon bits, cheese, croutons and creamy dressings.

- Pack lean protein such as tofu, fish, skinless chicken breast, beans and lentils.
- Pack cream-free, vegetable-based soups.
- Offer food in appropriate portions and, if you're worried that your child will be hungry, pack extra fruit and veggies.

2.

Vegetables
and Fruit

Children who consume the recommended
number of servings of vegetables and fruit tend
to have a higher intake of vitamins, minerals
and fibre—nutrients essential for healthy
growth and development. However, we know
that 70 per cent of Canadian children don't
eat the minimum recommended number of
servings per day.[12] To prevent your child from
falling short, aim to pack at least 1 fruit and
1 vegetable. Adding veggies to sandwiches
and dried fruit to cookies and bars is an easy
way to boost your child's intake.

When packing vegetables and fruit, make an effort to ensure they stay fresh, look appealing and are easily accessible. Although the whole fruit tends to stay the freshest, young children often struggle with peeling bananas and oranges, and they may prefer a cut apple over the whole fruit. Dipping apple slices into orange, pineapple or lemon juice slows the browning process and keeps the fruit looking fresh a little longer. Mixing fresh lemon or lime juice with avocado prevents it from browning.

Find out how your child likes her vegetables and make an effort to accommodate her preferences. Brenda used to find broccoli wrapped in the napkin of her daughter's lunch box. Ellie would devour broccoli at dinner but never touched it at school. This was when Brenda realized that Ellie preferred her broccoli steamed. If this is the case in your family, simply cook extra vegetables at dinner. There is no reason why leftover roasted potatoes or yams cannot be sent to school. Eaten with either fingers or forks, these vegetables are delicious dipped in tzatziki. Serving raw or steamed veggies with dip increases their appeal. For enticing dip recipes, see Chapter 4. Different fruit and vegetables contain different nutrients, so pack a daily variety and use the following charts for inspiration.

## Vegetables

| Vegetables | How to Prepare |
|---|---|
| Peppers: red, yellow, green and orange | Cut into strips and serve with dip, or slice thinly and add to sandwiches. |
| Potatoes: potatoes, yams | Pack mashed potatoes and sweet potatoes in a Thermos with leftover meat and gravy. Roasted potatoes can be eaten as is or with tzatziki for dipping. For those who have access to a microwave at school, jacket potatoes are always a hit (page 34). |
| Beets | Grate beets and add to sandwiches (page 43), or roast and serve with a fork or on a salad. |

| | |
|---|---|
| Cucumber | Slice cucumbers and add to sandwiches. Cut into chunks or seed and cut into strips. Try them with Homemade Hummus (page 97) for dipping. Or look for whole baby cucumbers. |
| Carrots | Carrots can be eaten raw, roasted or steamed. Grate them and add to sandwiches and salads. |
| Tomatoes | Cherry, grape and Campari tomatoes can be served whole. Seed and dice larger tomatoes and add to sandwiches or sprinkle on salads. |
| Radishes | Serve raw, whole or diced. Add to sandwiches and salads. |
| Green Beans | Trim and serve raw or steamed. |
| Broccoli | Cut into florets and serve raw or steamed. |
| Peas | Steam peas and serve as they are or sprinkled over salads. You can also mix them with other steamed veggies and pack in a Thermos over whole grain rice with a drizzle of soy sauce. |
| Celery | Serve raw celery plain or stuffed with cheese, hummus, or nut butters (page 32) if your school permits. Add diced celery to sandwich spreads. |
| Squash | Cut into cubes and roast. |
| Snap Peas | Trim ends, remove stringy bits and serve raw or dice and add to salads. |
| Snow Peas | Trim ends, remove stringy bits and serve raw. They can also be cut into strips and added to sandwiches or wraps. |
| Fennel | Cut into strips and serve raw. |
| Asparagus | Steam and serve either plain or wrapped with a piece of prosciutto or thinly sliced turkey. |
| Cauliflower | Cut into florets and serve with dip. |

TIP: Cut vegetables, stored in fresh water, will last in the refrigerator for several days. Doing this at the beginning of each week saves time in the morning and ensures your family has easy access to healthy snacks.

Vegetables and Fruit

## Cheese Stuffed Celery

This can be made the night before and stored in the refrigerator. Celery can also be filled with hummus, almond butter or peanut butter. If your child is attending a nut-free school, peanut butter-stuffed celery makes the perfect after-school snack. Try placing a few raisins on the peanut butter to make "ants on a log." For a change, try stuffing canned tuna or salmon in a stalk of celery.

I tbsp shredded Cheddar cheese
½ tbsp light cream cheese
I stalk celery, trimmed and cut in half crosswise

- In small bowl, combine Cheddar and cream cheese.
- With knife, fill celery with cheese mixture.

*Yield: Serves 1*

## Stuffed Cucumber Cups

Cucumber cups can be stuffed with a variety of fillings, including soft cheeses, canned fish and nut butters.

4 1½-inch cucumber slices
¼ cup Homemade Hummus (page 97) or store-bought
   equivalent

- With paring knife, and being careful not to cut through bottom of cucumber slices, cut gently around seeds.
- With small spoon, gently scoop out seeds, leaving ⅛-inch of cucumber at bottom of each cup.
- Stuff each cucumber cup with 1 tbsp of hummus.

*Yield: 4 cucumber cups*

## Colour Your World with Antioxidants

Antioxidants are plant-based chemical compounds. They are thought to neutralize free radicals, the natural by-product of metabolism. Free radicals can lead to a variety of life-threatening diseases, including cancer, heart disease and immune disorders. Some antioxidants give colour to fruit and vegetables. For example, beta carotene gives orange vegetables their colour, and the more orange a vegetable is, the more beta carotene it contains. Lycopenes give tomatoes and red peppers their colour, whereas anthocyanins give the blue-red hue to naturally purple foods, including berries, cabbage, purple potatoes and grapes. Lutein is a yellow-orange pigment found in corn, peas and leafy greens such as spinach and kale. Each of these pigments acts as a powerful antioxidant, playing an important biological role in the body.

To ensure your children reap the benefits of antioxidants, get them involved with packing their lunch boxes. In the evening, set out a variety of different coloured fruit and vegetables and make a game of it. Challenge your kids to see how many different colours they can pick. After all, we know children are more likely to eat food when they have been involved in choosing and preparing it.

## Edamame

Edamame, or soybeans, are an excellent source of protein. They can be prepared the night before and refrigerated.

**2 cups frozen edamame in their shells**
**½ tsp kosher salt (optional)**

- In large saucepan, bring 6 cups of water to boil.
- Add frozen edamame. Return water to boil and cook for another 3 to 5 minutes, or until edamame are tender.
- Rinse with cold running water to cool. Drain and refrigerate overnight.
- In the morning, sprinkle with salt if desired.

*Yield: Serves 2 to 3, depending on appetite*

Vegetables and Fruit

**The Power of Green**

Canada's Food Guide recommends that all Canadians eat at least 1 dark green vegetable per day. Dark green vegetables are an excellent source of folate, which is needed by rapidly dividing cells. Examples of dark green veggies are broccoli, green beans, peas and leafy greens. In fact, people who regularly consume leafy greens have a lower risk of diabetes, stroke, colon cancer, cataracts, bone loss and memory loss.[13] An easy way to include dark green vegetables in your child's lunch box is to add darker lettuces to sandwiches, salads and wraps. Instead of using iceberg lettuce, opt for romaine, arugula, green leaf lettuce, watercress and spinach.

# Jacket Potatoes

Some children have access to microwaves at school. For these kids, jacket potatoes make the perfect lunch, and the best part is they can be made and packed the night before. At school the children simply reheat the potatoes until they are warmed through and enjoy!

Children can personalize their potatoes by choosing their favourite veggie toppings. Brenda's son, Charlie, doesn't like corn, so he has his potato with broccoli and cheese. Her daughter, Ellie, prefers her potato with peas and cheese. Let your children choose the vegetables they enjoy.

Jacket potatoes can be prepared with a variety of different toppings, such as Black Bean Veggie Chili (page 160) or canned baked beans with a little shredded cheese. Yams and sweet potatoes are delicious prepared this way too.

## Veggie Jacket Potato

1 potato, baked
2 tsp non-hydrogenated margarine
2 rounded tbsp shredded Cheddar cheese
2 tbsp canned corn, drained and rinsed
2 broccoli florets, cooked and diced

- Cut top off potato and discard. Scoop out flesh, leaving enough potato around sides so it keeps its shape.
- In small bowl, mash potato flesh with margarine and 1 tbsp of cheese. Mix until cheese melts. Add corn and broccoli and combine.
- Scoop potato mixture back into potato skin and top with remaining tbsp of cheese. Place potato in reusable container and refrigerate overnight.

*Yield: Serves 1*

## Fruit

When sending soft fruit to school, be sure to pack it in a hard container to prevent bruising. Encourage your children to use the same container to bring their biodegradable waste home for composting.

| Fruit | How to Prepare |
|---|---|
| Melons: watermelon, honeydew and cantaloupe | Cut into cubes, balls or slices. |
| Mangoes | Wash but don't peel the mango. Slice mango lengthwise on either side of the pit. With a knife, score fruit on cut side in a criss-cross pattern. Place mango halves face down in a reusable container. To eat, flip mango inside out. |
| Papaya | Cut into slices, balls or cubes. Try with fresh lime juice. |
| Oranges: regular, tangerine, mandarin and clementine | Large oranges should be cut into sections for young children. Most young children should be able to peel mandarin oranges themselves. |
| Peaches, Nectarines, Pears and Plums | Best left whole but can be cut into segments for younger children. Tossing |

Vegetables and Fruit

| | |
|---|---|
| | the cut fruit with a little lemon juice should prevent browning. |
| **Avocados** | Works well as a sandwich spread when mixed with lemon or lime juice to prevent browning. |
| **Cherries** | Serve as they are, but because the pits can be a choking hazard, you may want to avoid giving them to younger children. |
| **Grapes** | Can be a choking hazard for young children. You may choose to cut them lengthwise into strips. |
| **Berries: strawberries, blueberries, raspberries, and blackberries** | Perfect for children of all ages—plus they contain more antioxidants than most other fruits and vegetables. |
| **Kiwis** | Peel and cut into slices or chunks. You can also cut the fruit in half and serve with a spoon for scooping out the flesh. |
| **Pineapples** | Cut into chunks or slices. They are also a delicious accompaniment to any fruit salad. |
| **Apples** | Serve whole or, for younger children, cut into segments. Toss cut fruit with a little lemon juice to prevent browning. |
| **Pomegranates** | These can be fiddly. Cut the fruit into quarters for older children and let them pick out the seeds. For young children, you should pick out the seeds before packing. You can also sprinkle the seeds over salad. |
| **Bananas** | Young children often have difficulty peeling bananas. To help them, top the banana at each end with a knife. Then make a slit along one of the seams and cut banana in half. |

| Dried Fruit: raisins, cranberries, apricots, peaches, apples and banana chips | Serve on its own, or add to trail mixes. Dried fruit can also be added to baked goods. |
| --- | --- |
| Canned fruit | Choose canned fruit that has been packed in juice rather than syrup. |

## Strawberry Applesauce

Rather than buying individually packaged containers of applesauce, make your own and freeze it in muffin tins. It's less expensive and easier on the environment. If your child prefers plain applesauce, simply omit the strawberries in this recipe.

4 medium apples, peeled, cored and quartered
12 strawberries, topped

- Place apples and strawberries in steamer basket and steam over boiling water until apples are soft, approximately 10 minutes. Let cool.
- Place apples and strawberries in bowl of food processor and purée until smooth. Pour into muffin tins and freeze. Once frozen, transfer to freezer-proof containers and store in freezer. To defrost, take portion out of freezer the night before and place in reusable container. In the morning, stir applesauce and pack.

*Yield: Serves 6*

## Roasted Fruit

This recipe can be made with a variety of fruit combinations. Try peaches and blueberries or apricots with raspberries. Served either on its own or with a dollop of yogurt, this simple dish is

Vegetables and Fruit

sure to please. Roasted fruit can be stored in the refrigerator for several days or frozen for later use.

**5 unblemished nectarines, halved and pits removed**
**25 raspberries**
**¼ cup granulated sugar**

- Preheat oven to 350°F.
- In shallow baking pan or gratin dish, place nectarines skin down in single layer, touching but not overlapping. Dot with raspberries and sprinkle with sugar.
- Place fruit in middle of oven and bake for 30 to 40 minutes, checking after 30 minutes. When done, fruit is tender and should have exuded its juices, leaving delicious syrup on bottom of dish. Roasted fruit will keep in refrigerator for several days.

*Yield: Serves 5*

## The Power of Orange

Canada's Food Guide recommends that all Canadians eat at least 1 orange vegetable per day. This is because orange vegetables like carrots, sweet potatoes, yams and squash are a good source of carotenoids, which the body converts into vitamin A. Vitamin A is essential for normal growth and development. As well as maintaining healthy vision, vitamin A helps the body boost immune function and fight infection. While most Canadian children get adequate amounts of vitamin A, the same cannot be said for adolescents. Recently it has come to light that approximately 40 per cent of Canadian children aged 14 to 18 years have an intake of vitamin A that falls below the estimated average requirement (EAR).[14]

To ensure this doesn't happen to your teen, serve a daily variety of orange fruits and vegetables. Because many orange-coloured fruits are also a good source of beta carotene, they can be served in place of orange vegetables. Such fruit includes papaya, mangoes, peaches,

Vegetables and Fruit

apricots and cantaloupe. Although oranges are a good source of folate and vitamin C, they aren't considered a good source of vitamin A and therefore cannot replace an orange vegetable. Keep this in mind when packing your child's lunch box and aim to include at least 1 orange fruit or vegetable.

## Fruit Filled Jell-O Fingers

Homemade Jell-O can be made with any combination of clear fruit juice and fresh fruit. Try white grape juice with raspberries or mandarin orange segments or perhaps purple grape juice with sliced strawberries or grapes. These Jell-O fingers can be packed in reusable containers and eaten with either fingers or forks.

4 sachets unflavoured gelatin
4 cups cranberry juice or other clear juice
1 cup blueberries or other small fruit (see suggestions above)

- In large bowl, sprinkle gelatin over 1 cup of cranberry juice and let stand for 2 minutes.
- In saucepan, heat remaining 3 cups of cranberry juice until just boiling. Pour over gelatin mixture and stir until dissolved. Pour into 8- x 8-inch pan, and gently scatter blueberries over mixture.
- Place Jell-O in refrigerator to set for approximately 3 hours or overnight.
- Briefly dip pan in hot water to loosen and flip Jell-O onto large plate or cutting board. With sharp knife, cut Jell-O into cubes or rectangles. You can even use cookie cutters to make fun shapes your kids will love! Jell-O should be refrigerated until ready to be eaten or packed with an ice pack.

*Yield: Serves 16*

Vegetables and Fruit

## Fruit Leather

Fruit leather contains some vitamin C and fibre, but because it is high in sugar, regular consumption of it increases the risk of developing cavities. From a dental perspective, the sticky consistency and high fructose content of fruit leather makes it no different than candy that sticks to your teeth (such as jujubes or toffee). Furthermore, the citric acid found in many fruit leathers corrodes the teeth, ultimately weakening the enamel. You wouldn't dream of sending your child to school with a daily bag of gumdrops, so it doesn't make sense to pack fruit leather every day. When eaten in moderation, fruit leather can be part of a healthy diet, but do encourage your children to brush their teeth after eating it.

# Fruit Pots

Perfect for young children, fruit pots contain an assortment of ready-to-eat fruit that can be eaten with either fingers or a fork. To make a fruit pot, pack a variety of different fruit in a reusable container. Choose from any combination of the following: mandarin orange segments, blueberries, strawberries, raspberries, blackberries, cherries, grapes, chunks of pineapple or kiwi, and cubes of melon. The night before, set out a variety of different fruit and get your kids to pack their own fruit pots. If adding sliced apples, pears or peaches, cut up these fruits in the morning and squeeze a little lemon juice over them to prevent browning. In a separate container, place some plain yogurt mixed with a drizzle of honey for dipping.

## Fruit for Life

A longitudinal study looking at 4,000 individuals concluded that those who ate the most fruit as children were 38 per cent less likely to develop cancer as adults.[15] To ensure your child is reaping the benefits of fruit, aim to serve at least 1 serving for breakfast and 1 serving for lunch. Put dried fruit in cookies, bars and other baked goods. Instead of offering a snack of crackers and cheese, provide a cheese and fruit platter.

3.

Sandwiches

One of the easiest ways to add variety to your child's lunch box is to use an assortment of different breads, such as pita pockets, buns, bagels, ciabatta, focaccia and wraps. Young children love things in mini, so look for mini bagels and pita pockets. One of the keys to making delicious sandwiches is choosing good quality bread. However, the healthiest breads do not contain preservatives and, as a result, tend to go stale quickly. To keep breads fresh, store them in the freezer. To thaw, either take the bread out the night before or lightly toast in the morning.

Make a concerted effort to choose whole grain bread. The consumption of whole grains has been linked to reduced risk of cardiovascular disease, obesity, diabetes and cancer.[16] Whole grain breads have not gone through the refining process, so all 3 components of the grain—the bran, germ and endosperm—remain intact. When grains are refined, the germ and bran are removed, which causes a loss of dietary fibre, B vitamins, minerals and antioxidants.

When choosing bread, read the listed ingredients carefully. Bread made from whole grains will have the word "whole" before the name of the grain. For example, good quality brown bread should be made with 100% whole wheat flour. Be warned: not all brown bread is made with whole grain flour. A dollop of molasses can turn any white bread brown. And just because bread is labelled "multi-grain" does not mean it is made with whole grain flour. Multi-grain simply means a variety of seeds and grains has been used. In fact, many multi-grain breads are made with the same kind of wheat flour that is used to make white bread.

Look for breads that contain at least 2 to 3 g of fibre per slice and recognizable ingredients such as whole grain flour, yeast, honey and salt. It's never a good sign when your bread is made with lots of strange sounding, polysyllabic ingredients.

It is important to make age-appropriate sandwiches that you know your children will enjoy. Young children are inclined to prefer smaller sandwiches with fewer ingredients. Not only are bulky sandwiches hard for them to grasp, they may have difficulty wrapping their mouths around them. Collect a variety of interesting cookie cutters and cut sandwiches into fun shapes that are the perfect size for little ones.

Be sensitive to your child's changing preferences. Although she may like tuna sandwiches at home, she may find them overpowering after the sandwich has been sitting in the cloakroom all morning. Learn how your child likes her sandwiches and make an effort to accommodate her tastes.

This chapter is divided into 4 sections: Pinwheels, Sandwiches, Pita Pockets and Souvlaki (made with pita bread), and Wraps. To ease the morning rush, all the recipes in this chapter outline what can be done the night before.

# Pinwheels

Pinwheels are appealing to young children, and almost any sandwich can be turned into a pinwheel. To make one, spread the sandwich filling over a small whole wheat tortilla and roll up tightly. If the pinwheel does not hold together, you can use a little cream cheese to seal it. Spread a ½-inch strip of cream cheese along one end of the tortilla. Roll up the tortilla starting with the opposite end and working toward the cream cheese, and press tightly. Using a sharp knife, slice into one-inch rounds.

Pinwheels can also be made with whole wheat bread. To do so, cut the crusts off a slice of bread and flatten it with a rolling pin. Spread the sandwich filling over the bread, roll it up and slice it into pinwheels. Young children may only eat 4 pinwheels and a few apple slices or a couple of grapes for lunch. It's always preferable for them to experience success with smaller portions than be overwhelmed by a big sandwich.

## SunButter and Jam Pinwheels

SunButter is the brand name of an organic sunflower seed butter. This recipe can be made with any seed, soy or nut butter, if your school permits. Prepare these pinwheels the night before and refrigerate overnight.

1 8-inch whole wheat soft flour tortilla
2 tbsp SunButter, or other seed, soy or nut butter
½ tbsp fruit-sweetened jam

• The night before, spread SunButter over tortilla. Spread

jam over SunButter and roll up. With a sharp knife, slice into 1-inch rounds, discarding ends. Pack in reusable container and refrigerate overnight.

*Yield: Serves 1 or 2 young children*

## Nut-Free Zones

An increase in life-threatening nut allergies has caused many schools to go "nut free." Some parents who have come to rely on peanut butter as a lunchtime staple may question whether their children are getting enough protein, but most North American children easily meet their daily protein requirement by eating a balanced diet containing foods from all 4 food groups. The following foods contain approximately the same amount of protein as 2 tbsp of peanut butter (which equals I serving of Meat and Alternatives): ¾ cup of yogurt, I oz/28g of cheese, I cup of milk and I oz/28 g of meat. The average slice of cheese pizza contains almost twice as much protein as 2 oz/56 g of peanut butter.

Peanut butter substitutes such as soy butter, which is made from toasted soybeans, and various seed butters, including sunflower and pumpkin seed butters, are also good and increasingly available sources of protein. If your child is reluctant to give up her favourite peanut butter sandwich, serve it for breakfast and pack her usual breakfast for lunch. There is no reason why she cannot enjoy whole grain cereal sprinkled with berries at lunch. Milk, packed in a pre-chilled Thermos, can be poured over the cereal at school.

## Cucumber Hummus Pinwheels

These make perfect bite-sized morsels for little hands.

2 tbsp Homemade Hummus (page 97) or your favourite store-bought equivalent
I 8-inch piece of cucumber, quartered lengthwise and seeded

1 8-inch whole wheat soft flour tortilla

- The night before, prepare hummus (if using) and cut up cucumber. Reserve 1 cucumber strip for pinwheel. The other 3 quarters can be cut into strips and packaged with other vegetables for tomorrow's lunch.
- In the morning, evenly spread hummus over tortilla.
- Place cucumber strip at one edge and roll up tightly. With sharp knife, slice into 1-inch rounds, discarding ends. Pack in reusable container.

*Yield: Serves 1 or 2 young children*


## Turkey and Swiss Cheese Pinwheels

These are quick to whip up and can be made either the night before or in the morning. Instead of the turkey and Swiss cheese, you can use ham and Cheddar cheese. Or use whatever meat you have on hand, slicing it as thinly as possible.

1 tbsp light cream cheese
1 8-inch whole wheat soft flour tortilla
1 tsp mustard (optional)
2 tbsp shredded Swiss cheese
2 thin slices cooked turkey, torn into pieces

- The night before, evenly spread cream cheese over tortilla. Spread mustard (if using) over cream cheese and evenly scatter with cheese and turkey. Roll up tightly. With sharp knife, slice into 1-inch rounds, discarding ends. Pack in reusable container and refrigerate overnight.

*Yield: Serves 1 or 2 young children*

Sandwiches

## Salmon Salad Pinwheels

Substitute canned tuna for the salmon in this recipe, if you like.

½ can (7½ oz/213 g) salmon, drained and skin removed
1 tbsp mayonnaise
1 8-inch stalk celery, quartered lengthwise
1 8-inch whole wheat soft flour tortilla
½ tsp light cream cheese

- The night before, in small bowl, combine salmon and mayonnaise. Prepare celery, reserving 1 celery stick for pinwheel. The remaining celery can be cut into sticks and packed with other vegetables for tomorrow's lunch. Refrigerate salmon mixture and celery overnight.
- In the morning, evenly spread salmon mixture over tortilla, leaving a 1-inch border around tortilla. Place celery at one end of tortilla. Spread cream cheese on opposite end in ½-inch strip. Starting with end of tortilla with celery, roll up tightly, working toward cream cheese end, and press tightly so that cream cheese "glues" pinwheel together. With sharp knife, slice into 1-inch rounds, discarding ends. Pack in reusable container.

*Yield: Serves 1 or 2 young children*

## Christina's Cranberry Pinwheels

These pinwheels can be made with any combination of dried fruit. Just substitute ¼ cup of your child's favourite dried fruit for the cranberries and apricots.

2 tbsp light cream cheese
1 8-inch whole wheat soft flour tortilla
5 dried apricots, diced
2 tbsp dried cranberries

- The night before, evenly spread cream cheese over tortilla. Scatter apricots and cranberries over tortilla and roll up tightly. With sharp knife, slice into 1-inch rounds, discarding ends. Pack in reusable container and refrigerate overnight.

*Yield: Serves 1 or 2 young children*

## Mexican Black Bean Pinwheels

These pinwheels are best served with salsa on the side for dipping.

2 tbsp light cream cheese
1 8-inch whole wheat soft flour tortilla
2 tbsp canned black beans, drained and rinsed
2 tbsp diced sweet red pepper
1/3 cup shredded Cheddar cheese
1/3 cup mild salsa

- The night before, spread cream cheese evenly over tortilla. Scatter beans, red pepper and cheese over tortilla and roll up tightly. With sharp knife, slice into 1-inch rounds, discarding ends. Pack pinwheels and salsa in separate reusable containers and refrigerate overnight.

*Yield: Serves 1 or 2 young children*

## Sandwiches

### Salmon Salad Bunwich with Caper Dill Mayonnaise

This sandwich is rich in calcium because it contains both canned salmon (with bones) and watercress—good sources of calcium. This recipe makes enough sandwich filling for 2 to 3 sandwiches,

Sandwiches

depending on appetite and the size of the bun.

    1 can (7½ oz/213 g) salmon, drained and skin removed
    1 rounded tbsp mayonnaise
    1 rounded tbsp finely diced red onion (optional)
    2 tsp capers
    1 rounded tsp chopped fresh dill
    1 tsp fresh lemon juice
    1 whole grain bun, cut in half horizontally
    ½ cup chopped watercress

- The night before, combine salmon, mayonnaise, red onion (if using), capers, dill and lemon juice and refrigerate overnight.
- In the morning, spread bottom half of bun with half salmon mixture. Top with watercress and remaining half of bun. Cut sandwich in half and pack in reusable container. Extra filling can either be refrigerated for tomorrow's lunch or used for additional sandwich.

*Yield: Serves 1*

## The ABCs of Omega-3s

Omega-3 fatty acids are essential nutrients. Our bodies cannot make them in sufficient quantity to meet our physiological needs and so they must be supplied by our diet. Omega-3 fatty acids are highly concentrated in the brain and appear to be particularly important for cognitive, behavioural and cardiovascular function.

There are 3 main types of omega-3 fatty acids: eicosapentaenoic acid (EPA), docosahexaenoic acid (DHA) and alpha-linolenic acid (ALA). Fish is the best source of omega-3 fatty acids as it contains both DHA and EPA, the 2 types of omega-3 fatty acids that are readily used by the body and particularly important for cognitive function. For this reason a healthy diet should contain at least 2 servings of fish per week. ALA comes from plant-based sources such as flaxseeds, walnuts and canola oil. When ALA is eaten, the body converts it into EPA and DHA. However, this conversion is not done very efficiently, so it is best to obtain DHA and EPA directly from fish.

Because of their beneficial properties, omega-3 fatty acids are increasingly being added to a variety of foods, including orange juice, milk, cheese and yogurt. When purchasing these foods, try to find those fortified with fish oil DHA and/or EPA as opposed to ALA. This is especially important for children who do not eat fish regularly.

## Egg Salad Bunwich

Eggs have a fairly delicate flavour and can be overpowered by the green onion in this recipe, so it's best to wait till the last minute to add it.

1 hard-boiled egg, chopped
1 tbsp mayonnaise
10 thin slices of green onion (optional)
1 whole wheat roll, cut in half horizontally
1 leaf green leaf lettuce, torn in half

- The night before, in a small bowl, combine eggs and mayonnaise and refrigerate overnight.
- In the morning, add onions (if using) to egg mixture and stir to combine. Spread egg mixture over bottom half of roll. Top with lettuce and remaining half of roll. Cut sandwich in half and pack in reusable container.

*Yield: Serves 1*

Sandwiches

## Tips for Preventing Soggy Sandwiches

- Pack tomatoes and other moist ingredients separately, as they can seep into the bread and make it soggy. Alternatively, you can seed and dice tomatoes before adding them to sandwiches.
- Use dry ingredients. Make sure any lettuce and other vegetables are thoroughly dry after washing.
- Put a layer of dried lettuce next to the bread and then put your sandwich filling, sauce or mayonnaise on top of the lettuce so it doesn't seep into the bread.
- Lightly toast the bread or bun first to make it less susceptible to seepage.
- Add crispy vegetables to sandwiches. Try celery, cucumber, carrots, radishes or pickles. Use shredded cabbage instead of lettuce.
- Make sandwiches with frozen bread. The bread is less likely to absorb the filling and will be thawed by lunch. Using frozen bread also helps to keep your sandwich cold.
- If your child is particularly sensitive to soggy sandwiches, you may have to pack the filling separately.
- Spread the bread with a little non-hydrogenated margarine before adding moist ingredients. The margarine acts as a barrier.

## Roast Beef Bagel

Cook extra roast beef for dinner so that you can make this sandwich for lunch the next day.

1 whole grain bagel, cut in half horizontally
2 thin slices cooked roast beef
$1/2$ tsp Dijon mustard (or yellow mustard if your child prefers)
$1/2$ tsp mayonnaise
$1/4$ tsp horseradish (optional)
4 thin slices cucumber
2 slices tomato, seeded and cut into strips
1 leaf romaine lettuce, torn into smaller pieces
1 thin slice red onion (optional)

1 slice aged Cheddar cheese
Kosher salt and freshly ground pepper

- The night before, organize ingredients and refrigerate.
- In the morning, toast bagel lightly.
- Place roast beef on bottom half of bagel. Thinly spread mustard, mayonnaise and horseradish (if using) over meat. Top with cucumber, tomatoes, lettuce, red onion (if using) and cheese. Sprinkle with salt and pepper to taste, and top with remaining half of bagel. Cut sandwich in half and pack in reusable container.

*Yield: Serves 1*

## Luncheon Meats

Cold cuts or luncheon meats have long been a lunchroom staple. Although convenient, the vast majority of these meats are high in sodium, fat and chemical preservatives and should not be the mainstay of your child's lunch. In fact, a typical serving of deli meat contains as much as 30 per cent of an adult's daily sodium intake and 25 per cent of his fat intake. This is significant considering that the meat is only part of the sandwich filling. For a healthier alternative, substitute home-cooked meat in sandwiches. To do so, cook extra meat (chicken, turkey, beef, lamb or pork) with dinner. Properly cooked, leftover meat can be safely stored in the refrigerator for several days. Alternatively, you can divide the meat into individual portions and freeze for future use. To defrost, remove the meat from the freezer the night before and place it in the refrigerator. It will be ready to use by morning.

You can also look for nitrate-free alternatives, which are available at many artisanal butchers across Canada. Because these meats do not contain preservatives, they will not keep as long as regular deli meats and should be used within a couple of days.

Sandwiches

## Veggie Tuna Bagel

Young children tend to prefer simple flavours and foods with fewer ingredients, whereas older children are more adventurous. In this recipe you can add all the suggested vegetables or just a couple. Pick the ones your child likes, or even better, get him to choose the veggies and make the sandwich himself! Remember, children are more likely to eat a meal when they have been involved in preparing it.

I can (6 oz/170 g) low-sodium, light tuna, drained
½ cup mixed vegetables, such as grated carrot, corn, diced
    celery, diced radishes and diced sweet red pepper
I tbsp chopped fresh cilantro
2 tsp finely diced red onion or green onion (optional)
I rounded tbsp mayonnaise
2 whole wheat bagels, cut in half horizontally
8 slices cucumber
2 handfuls arugula

- The night before, combine tuna, your choice of vegetables, cilantro, onion (if using) and mayonnaise. Refrigerate overnight.
- In the morning, lightly toast bagels.
- Spread tuna mixture on bottom halves of bagels. Top with cucumber, arugula and remaining halves of bagels. Cut sandwiches in half and pack in reusable containers.

*Yield: Serves 2*

### Canned Tuna

A tuna sandwich is a healthy lunch and a good way to boost your child's intake of omega-3 fatty acids. However, if your child eats tuna daily, she runs the risk of developing mercury toxicity, which can cause damage to the central nervous system and even death. Symptoms of mercury toxicity include memory loss, loss of concentration, numbness and/or tingling in the hands and feet, depression and possible sensory impairment, such as diminished vision, hearing or speech.

Mercury accumulates in the food chain, and therefore larger predatory fish such as albacore tuna have higher mercury levels. Because of this, Health Canada recommends that young children between the ages of 1 and 4 years eat no more than 1 Food Guide serving (75 g, 2½ oz, ½ cup) per week and that children between the ages of 5 and 11 eat no more than 2 Food Guide servings per week.[17] At present there are no restrictions on canned light tuna as it is made with smaller fish (such as skipjack, yellowfin and tongol). Due to their smaller body mass, children are more susceptible than adults to toxicity. Therefore it makes sense to choose canned light tuna whenever possible and not to exceed Health Canada's recommendations for consumption.

## Lox and Cream Cheese Bagel

If you are making this sandwich for younger children, try to find mini bagels—which are always a hit—and adjust portions accordingly.

1 bagel, cut in half horizontally
1½ tbsp light cream cheese
2 thin slices smoked salmon
1 thin slice red onion (optional)
1 tsp capers

- The night before, organize ingredients and refrigerate.
- In the morning, toast bagel lightly.
- Spread cream cheese evenly over bagel, top with salmon and onion (if using) and sprinkle with capers. Top with remaining half of bagel. Cut sandwich in half and pack in reusable container.

*Yield: Serves 1*

Sandwiches

## Listeriosis and Luncheon Meats

Concern over the safety of luncheon meats spiked after the 2008 listeriosis outbreak in Canada. *Listeria monocytogenes* (listeria) is a type of bacteria that can cause a rare but serious illness called listeriosis. The outbreak originated in a meat processing plant in Toronto. Twenty-three Canadians died and 57 became seriously ill.[18]

For many, this crisis was the catalyst to look for safer and healthier alternatives to cold cuts. By switching to home-cooked meat you can avoid the preservatives as well as the high sodium and fat content of most processed meats. To minimize your risk of contracting listeriosis or other food-borne illnesses, make sure meat, poultry and fish are thoroughly cooked. Although it is best to eat leftovers within 24 hours, properly cooked meat and fish can be safely stored in the refrigerator for several days.

If you continue to serve deli meat occasionally, you can reduce your risk of contracting listeriosis by reheating both deli meat and hot dogs until steaming hot (microwave on high for approximately 10 to 12 seconds). If you want to eat the meat cold, refrigerate it after heating, but do not use the original packaging. Never eat hot dogs straight from the package, and be sure to carefully discard the fluid from the hot dog package because it may contain bacteria. You can further minimize your risk of infection by choosing salted and dried deli meat, such as pepperoni and salami, which is less likely to support the growth of bacteria.

## Smoked Paprika Mayonnaise

1/3 cup mayonnaise
3/4 tbsp smoked paprika

• In small bowl, combine mayonnaise and paprika.

*Yield: 3/4 cup*

## Tortilla Bocadillo

This potato omelette sandwich, or *bocadillo de tortilla* as it is called in Spain, is traditionally served with Smoked Paprika Mayonnaise. It is a little spicy, so if you are making this sandwich for young children, you may want to use regular mayonnaise instead.

2 triangular shaped wedges of Spanish Omelette (page 161),
cut so they fit side by side in rectangle shape on baguette
1 tbsp Smoked Paprika Mayonnaise (page 56)
1 6-inch piece of baguette, cut in half horizontally
1 handful baby spinach

- The night before, prepare Spanish Omelette (or make it on the weekend for a perfect family brunch and save leftovers) and Smoked Paprika Mayonnaise and refrigerate.
- In the morning, spread Smoked Paprika Mayonnaise on each side of baguette. Place omelette segments on one half of baguette, top with spinach and other half of baguette. Cut sandwich in half and pack in reusable container.

*Yield: Serves 1*

## Santa Fe Chicken Bagel

This sandwich is likely to appeal to older children or those with more sophisticated palates.

1 bagel, cut in half horizontally
¼ avocado
1 squeeze fresh lime juice
1¼ oz/35 g chicken breast, cooked and thinly sliced
1 rounded tsp Smoked Paprika Mayonnaise (page 56)
1 slice sweet yellow or red pepper
1 slice tomato, seeded and cut into strips
1 leaf romaine lettuce, halved

Sandwiches

- The night before, organize ingredients and prepare Smoked Paprika Mayonnaise. Refrigerate overnight.
- In the morning, lightly toast bagel.
- Mash avocado with lime juice and spread evenly over one half of bagel. Top with chicken.
- Spread Smoked Paprika Mayonnaise on chicken and top with yellow pepper, tomatoes, lettuce and remaining half of bagel. Cut sandwich in half and pack in reusable container.

*Yield: Serves 1*

## Shrimp Sandwich

This sandwich can be made with any type of bread and is also delicious with a few slices of avocado. If you're not serving it immediately, mash a little lemon or lime juice with the avocado to prevent it from browning.

½ cup peeled cooked shrimp
1 tomato, seeded and diced
1 rounded tbsp mayonnaise
2 tsp cocktail sauce
1 tsp chopped fresh parsley (optional)
4 slices whole wheat bread
1 large handful arugula

- The night before, in small bowl, combine shrimp, tomatoes, mayonnaise, cocktail sauce and parsley (if using) and refrigerate overnight.
- In the morning, lightly toast bread. Spread shrimp mixture on 2 slices of bread and top with arugula and remaining slices of bread. Cut sandwiches in half and pack in reusable containers.

*Yield: Serves 2*

## Does Fish Consumption Lower the Risk of Depression?

It has long been suggested that the omega-3 fatty acids in fish play a role in reducing the symptoms of depression in adults. Recently, a study looking at adolescents showed an association between higher fish intake and lower rates of depression in teenage boys.[19]

## Cucumber Sandwich

This simple sandwich is ideal for young children. Dig out the cookie cutters to create a tantalizing treat. For variety you can add a few slices of sweet red pepper and/or romaine lettuce.

2 slices whole wheat bread
1 tsp non-hydrogenated margarine
2 tsp mayonnaise
8 slices of cucumber, thinly sliced
Kosher salt and freshly ground pepper (optional)

- The night before, organize ingredients and refrigerate.
- In the morning, lightly toast bread slices and spread with margarine.
- Spread 1 slice of bread with mayonnaise and top with cucumbers. Sprinkle lightly with salt and pepper to taste (if using) and top with remaining slice of bread. Use cookie cutters to cut out fun shapes and pack in reusable container.

*Yield: Serves 1*

Sandwiches

## Chili Mayonnaise

Chili Mayonnaise is an ingredient in our Flank Steak Sandwich below and is also delicious in chicken salad sandwiches.

2 tbsp mayonnaise
I tsp Asian garlic chili sauce or sweet chili sauce

- In small bowl, combine ingredients thoroughly.

*Yield: Approximately 2 tbsp*

## Flank Steak Sandwich

Ciabatta is a crusty bread that goes well with roast beef and steak sandwiches. If you cannot find the individual buns, buy a loaf and cut it into slices. Foccacia also works well with beef sandwiches.

4 thin slices Barbecued Asian Flank Steak (page 162)
2 tsp Chili Mayonnaise (above)
I ciabatta bun, cut in half horizontally
I large handful arugula
6 slices cucumber
2 thin slices sweet red pepper
I to 2 slices mozzarella cheese (optional)

- The day before, prepare Barbecued Asian Flank Steak for dinner and refrigerate leftovers. Prepare Chili Mayonnaise and organize ingredients. Refrigerate overnight.
- In the morning, spread one half of bun with Chili Mayonnaise. Top with arugula and then slices of Barbecued Asian Flank Steak, cucumber, red pepper, cheese (if using), and remaining half of bun. Cut sandwich in half and pack in reusable container.

*Yield: Serves 1*

## Homemade Pesto

Pesto is useful to have on hand. It can be tossed with pasta to make Kid's Pesto Pasta Salad (page 134) or used in a variety of different sandwiches. If your school is nut-free, simply omit the pine nuts—the pesto is delicious this way too! Extra pesto can be frozen in ice cube trays.

1 ½ cups packed fresh basil leaves
1 cup grated Parmesan cheese
½ cup pine nuts (optional)
2 garlic cloves
2 to 4 tbsp extra-virgin olive oil

- In bowl of food processor, process basil, Parmesan, pine nuts (if using) and garlic until finely minced. With processor running, slowly pour olive oil through feed tube and process until smooth consistency is reached.

*Yield: Approximately 2 cups*

## Chicken Pesto Ciabatta

You can replace the ciabatta bun in this recipe with a whole wheat tortilla and turn it into a wrap. If you do, use the lettuce as a barrier between the tortilla and the rest of the ingredients so the wrap doesn't get soggy.

1 small tomato, seeded and diced
2 oz/56 g cooked chicken breast, thinly sliced
1 tbsp Homemade Pesto (above), or your favourite store-bought equivalent
1 ciabatta bun, cut in half horizontally
1 tsp mayonnaise
1 large leaf green leaf lettuce, torn in half
¼ avocado
1 squeeze fresh lemon or lime juice

Sandwiches

- The night before, seed and dice tomato, cook chicken breast and organize rest of ingredients. Refrigerate overnight.
- In the morning, spread pesto evenly on bottom half of bun. Top with chicken. Spread mayonnaise on chicken and top with lettuce and tomatoes.
- In small bowl, mash avocado with lemon juice and spread on top half of bun. Place on top of tomatoes. Cut sandwich in half and pack in reusable container.

*Yield: Serves 1*

## Ellie's Lunch Box Pizzas

These are always a hit with Brenda's daughter, Ellie. As an added benefit, they can be made and packed the night before. For variety, try different toppings such as thinly sliced mushrooms, thinly sliced zucchini, finely diced pineapple, diced cooked chicken and a little feta cheese. Get your kids to choose their own toppings.

I whole wheat English muffin, cut in half horizontally
2 rounded tsp tomato paste
2 very thin slices sweet red or yellow pepper
3 tbsp shredded Cheddar cheese
2 cherry tomatoes, thinly sliced

- The night before, toast English muffin to prevent sogginess.
- Thinly spread tomato paste on each half of English muffin and top with red pepper and cheese. Place 2 to 4 slices of tomato on each pizza.
- Place pizzas directly on oven rack and broil until cheese bubbles and pizzas begin to brown around edges. Placing pizzas on rack helps keep crust crisp. Lay baking sheet on rack below to catch dripping cheese.
- Lay pizzas on wire rack to cool. Pizzas must be completely

cool before packing to avoid condensation from forming inside container.
• Pack in reusable container and refrigerate overnight.

*Yield: Serves 1*

## Should I Be Concerned about the Presence of Hormones in Our Food Supply?

Although banned in Europe, hormones are routinely given to beef cattle in both Canada and the United States to speed up their growth and increase lean body tissue. Although Health Canada states growth hormones do not pose a threat to human health,[20] some scientists remain concerned. They worry hormonal residue in the meat could potentially disturb hormonal balances in the body. Some fear this may contribute to an earlier onset of puberty for girls.

While these fears are primarily theoretical, it makes sense to avoid food that contains hormones, especially for growing children. Consider buying organic beef, which is raised without the use of hormones or antibiotics. Alternatively, substitute ground turkey or chicken in recipes. Not only is poultry reared without hormones, ground poultry is also leaner than ground beef. In Canada, hormones are not used in the production of lamb, pork, poultry or dairy cattle. Recombinant bovine somatotropin (rBST), a synthetic hormone, is given to dairy cattle in the United States to speed up their milk production. It has never been approved for sale in Canada. If you are in the habit of cross-border shopping or buying American dairy products, you may want to reconsider.

Sandwiches

## The Sausage Hot Dog

The quality of sausage meat varies significantly. Read labels or talk to your butcher to find out what is in the sausages you buy. Choose one that contains a higher percentage of meat and ingredients such as herbs, spices and bread crumbs. If the ingredient list is long and there are a lot of strange-sounding additives, give the sausage a pass.

The topping options in this recipe are merely suggestions. Find out what your child likes with his sausage and pack accordingly.

Children who have access to microwaves may choose to reheat their sausage at school. If a cold sausage doesn't appeal, try sending bangers and mash. To do so, prepare extra mashed potatoes for dinner and cook the sausage the night before. In the morning, simply reheat the potatoes and sausage. Cut the sausage into chunks and pack them in a Thermos over the mashed potatoes.

1 good quality turkey sausage
1 whole wheat hot dog bun, cut in half horizontally

Topping Options:
Shredded Cheddar cheese
Sautéed onions (which can be made the night before)
Ketchup
Mustard
Relish

- The night before, cook sausage, let cool and refrigerate. Pack selected toppings and refrigerate overnight.
- In the morning, cut bun in half. Place sausage next to bun and pack in reusable container.
- At school, your child will place hot dog in bun and dress with desired toppings.

*Yield: Serves 1*

## More Sandwiches

In addition to our many sandwich recipes, you may want to try some of the following filling combinations.

**Cream cheese with 1 or 2 of the following options:** sliced cucumber, sliced sweet red pepper, mashed avocado with a squeeze of lime juice, seeded and diced tomatoes, a selection of chopped dried fruit, fruit-sweetened jam, mashed sardines mixed with ketchup, and lettuce.

**Hummus with 1 or 2 of the following options:** sliced cucumber, shredded Cheddar cheese, seeded and diced tomatoes, sliced sweet red pepper, lettuce, grated carrot and grated beet

**Tuna and mayonnaise with 1 or 2 of the following options:** corn, green onions, ketchup, diced celery, diced radishes, shredded cheese, sliced cucumber, grated carrot, diced sweet red pepper and any of the dark lettuces

**Peanut butter or almond butter (if your school permits) or sunflower seed butter with 1 or 2 of the following options:** sliced banana, fruit-sweetened jam, raisins or other diced dried fruit, grated carrot, lettuce, crispy bacon and diced apple

**Any sliced cheese with mustard and/or mayonnaise and one or 2 of the following options:** grated carrot, grated beet, lettuce, seeded and diced tomatoes, sliced cucumber, sliced sweet red pepper, avocado mashed with fresh lime juice, sliced pickles, and your choice of leftover meat (ham, chicken, turkey, pork or beef)

**Canned salmon and mayonnaise with 1 or 2 of the following options:** ketchup, green onions, diced celery, corn, sliced cucumber, diced radishes, lettuce, shredded cheese and grated carrot

**Shredded Cheddar cheese** with relish and grated beet and/or grated carrot

**Hard-boiled egg** mashed with mayonnaise and crumbled bacon and/or seeded and diced tomatoes, diced celery and/or diced sweet red pepper

**Cooked shredded turkey or chicken** with cranberry sauce, mayonnaise and lettuce; or mango chutney, lettuce and sliced cucumber

**Leftover grilled vegetables** (zucchini, sweet red pepper, eggplant) with spinach, goat cheese and pesto

Sandwiches

TIP: If your child likes peanut butter and banana sandwiches (or sunflower seed and banana sandwiches), consider packing the banana separately as sliced banana goes mushy if it sits in the cloakroom all morning long. To avoid this, pack a dull knife so that your child can slice and add the banana to her sandwich at school.

# Pita Pockets and Souvlaki

The following sandwiches are made with pita bread. Pita bread can be cut in half to create 2 pita pockets that can be opened and filled, or it can be stuffed and rolled like a souvlaki. When making a souvlaki, place lettuce in the pita to act as a barrier between the bread and the meat and tzatziki. The lettuce prevents the sauce from seeping into the pita and making the sandwich soggy. Always pack souvlaki seam down so it doesn't unroll.

If you find pita bread difficult to open, simply heat it in the microwave for 20 seconds. Once heated, it should open with ease.

## Lamb Meatball Souvlaki

This is a perfect sandwich for lunch and dinner. At Brenda's house the adults enjoy it with a few drops of hot sauce. It is also good with hummus and sliced pickles.

> 3 to 4 Lamb Meatballs (page 85), depending on appetite
> 2 tbsp Minted Tzatziki (page 97) or your favourite store-bought equivalent
> 1 whole wheat pita pocket
> 2 large leaves green leaf lettuce
> 2 tbsp seeded and diced tomato

- The night before, prepare Lamb Meatballs and Minted Tzatziki (if using) and refrigerate overnight.
- In the morning, slit top of pita pocket with knife and gently open. Place 1 lettuce leaf inside. Place meatballs on top of

lettuce. Drizzle tzatziki on top of meatballs and top with tomatoes. Tear remaining lettuce leaf into bite-sized pieces and place on top of tomatoes. Wrap tightly to enclose filling and place seam side down in reusable container.

*Yield: Serves 1*

## Salmon Souvlaki Pita

3 Mini Salmon Patties (page 93)
2 tbsp Dilled Tzatziki (page 97) or store-bought alternative
2 large leaves green leaf lettuce
I whole wheat pita pocket

- The night before, prepare Mini Salmon Patties and Dilled Tzatziki (if using) and refrigerate overnight.
- In the morning, slit top of pita pocket with knife and gently open. Place 1 lettuce leaf inside pita pocket. Place salmon patties on top of lettuce and drizzle with tzatziki. Tear remaining lettuce leaf into bite-sized pieces and stuff into pita. Wrap tightly to enclose filling. Place seam side down in reusable container.

*Yield: Serves 1*

## Dilly Delicious Tuna Pita Pocket
This is a yummy alternative to an old-fashioned tuna sandwich.

I can (6 oz/170 g) low-sodium, light tuna, drained
I rounded tbsp mayonnaise
I squeeze fresh lemon juice
I tbsp finely diced red onion (optional)
I large dill pickle, diced

Sandwiches

½ rounded tsp chopped fresh dill
Freshly ground pepper
1 whole wheat pita pocket
2 large leaves green leaf lettuce
6 slices cucumber

- The night before, combine tuna, mayonnaise, lemon juice, onion (if using), pickle and dill. Add pepper to taste, and refrigerate overnight.
- In the morning, cut pita in half and gently open up pockets. Place 1 lettuce leaf inside each pita pocket. Divide tuna mixture evenly between pita pockets and top with cucumber slices. Pack in reusable container.

*Yield: Serves 1 (for young children, half a pita will suffice)*

## Greek Pita Pocket

If you don't have pita bread, the following sandwich can be made with whole wheat bread or a whole grain bagel. Serve this sandwich with Minted Tzatziki (page 97) and vegetable sticks for dipping.

¼ cup Homemade Hummus (page 97) or your favourite store-bought equivalent
10 slices cucumber
8 strips of sweet red pepper
8 strips of sweet green pepper
1 tsp red onion, finely diced
½ tomato, seeded and diced
1 dill pickle, sliced
1 whole wheat pita pocket
2 large leaves green leaf lettuce
¼ cup crumbled feta cheese

- The night before, prepare Homemade Hummus (if using) and refrigerate. Slice or chop cucumber, red and green peppers, onion, tomatoes and pickle and refrigerate overnight.
- In the morning, cut pita in half and gently open up pockets. Line each pocket with 1 lettuce leaf and spread with hummus. Stuff cucumber, red and green peppers, onion, tomatoes and pickle into each pocket and sprinkle with feta cheese. Pack in reusable containers.

*Yield: Serves 1 (for young children, half a pita will suffice)*

## The Power of Presentation

For young children, the school day is long and a packed lunch can represent a little comfort from home. Make an effort to personalize your children's lunch boxes. Get their help in selecting a lunch kit and water bottle they like. Personal touches like a well-placed sticker of their favourite cartoon character, a joke or a note are sure to bring a smile to any child's face. If your child has a test or is competing in a sporting event, be sure to include a good luck message. Adding the occasional novelty item such as a pen or pencil is always a fun surprise.

Your child's lunch should look appealing as well as taste good. Choose colourful fruits and vegetables that look enticing together. Use cookie cutters to perk up boring sandwiches. After all, the more attractive a lunch looks, the more likely it is to be eaten.

## Wraps

A wrap is perfect for someone with a big appetite, since a lot can be packed into it. Another benefit of a wrap is that soft flour tortillas are less likely to get soggy than other types of bread. A large piece of romaine or green leaf lettuce works well as a barrier between the sandwich filling and the tortilla. Instead of using foil or cling wrap to hold your wrap together, try spreading a ½-inch

Sandwiches

strip of cream cheese along one end of the wrap. Starting with the other end, roll the wrap toward the cream cheese and press tightly. The cream cheese will act as "glue" to seal the wrap together, eliminating the need for foil or plastic wrap (and the resulting waste). You'll need the larger size of tortillas to make these wraps.

## Mango Chicken Curry Wrap

This wrap is perfect for your adventurous eater!

| | |
|---|---|
| ⅓ cup diced cooked chicken | ⅓ cup diced mango |
| 4 radishes, diced | 2 large leaves romaine lettuce |
| ½ stalk celery, diced | 2 10-inch whole wheat soft flour tortillas |
| 1 tbsp mayonnaise | |
| 1 tbsp low-fat plain yogurt | 2 handfuls arugula |
| 1 tsp tomato paste | ½ tsp cream cheese |
| 1 tsp medium curry powder | |

- The night before, in small bowl, combine chicken, radishes, celery, mayonnaise, yogurt, tomato paste and curry powder and refrigerate overnight.
- In the morning, add mango to chicken mixture and stir to combine.
- Place 1 lettuce leaf in centre of each tortilla. Spread 8-inch vertical strip of chicken mixture along centre of each lettuce leaf and top with arugula.
- Spread ½-inch strip of cream cheese along right-hand end of tortilla.
- Wrap lettuce around filling, then fold 1½-inch bottom end of tortilla toward centre, and roll up tightly from left toward cream cheese edge, pressing to seal. Repeat with second wrap. Place seam side down in reusable containers.

*Yield: Serves 2*

## Do Foods Cause Hyperactivity?

Contrary to popular belief, sugar does not cause hyperactivity. In fact, it actually has the opposite effect. Sugar causes the release of serotonin, which has a calming effect on the body and actually helps us sleep. But many foods that contain a lot of sugar are also high in a number of chemical additives that may contribute to hyperactivity in sensitive children. These additives include a group of chemical preservatives called benzoates, as well as 4 artificial colours (tartrazine, ponceau, sunset yellow and carmoisine). These additives may be listed on labels as "preservatives" and "artificial colour," since there is currently no regulation requiring they be listed by name.

Some common foods known to contain these benzoates and artificial colours include boxed macaroni and cheese, candy, chewing gum, soda pop, yogurt, jam and jelly, canned soup, sauces including barbecue, soy and teriyaki, as well as some convenience food mixes such as pudding and cake mixes. Caffeine, a naturally occurring compound found in chocolate, is another stimulant known to cause hyperactivity in sensitive children.

Chemical additives are just one more reason to keep processed foods out of the lunch box and to pack a healthy variety of whole foods instead.

## Black Bean Turkey Taco Wrap

Black Bean Turkey Tacos (page 151) are a favourite dinner at Brenda's house, and the best part is that leftovers can be turned into wraps for lunch the next day. In fact, the entire wrap can be assembled the night before and refrigerated overnight.

Sandwiches

   1 large leaf green leaf lettuce
   1 10-inch whole wheat soft flour tortilla
   3 tbsp Black Bean Turkey Taco mixture (page 151), chilled
   2 tbsp shredded Cheddar cheese
   2 tbsp seeded and diced tomatoes (optional)
   ½ tsp light cream cheese
   2 tbsp salsa

- The night before, place lettuce in centre of tortilla. Spread Black Bean Turkey Taco mixture in 8-inch vertical strip in centre of lettuce. Top with cheese and tomatoes (if using).
- Spread ½-inch strip of cream cheese along right-hand end of tortilla.
- Wrap lettuce around filling, then fold 1½-inch bottom and top ends of tortilla toward centre, and roll up tightly from left toward cream cheese edge, pressing to seal. Place seam side down in reusable container.
- Pack salsa in separate reusable container so that the wrap can be dipped at school.

*Yield: Serves 1*

## Basil Mayonnaise

Basil mayonnaise is a delicious alternative to regular mayonnaise and a lovely complement to chicken, shrimp and vegetable sandwiches.

¼ cup mayonnaise
1 tbsp finely chopped fresh basil
1 squeeze fresh lemon juice

- In small bowl, combine ingredients thoroughly.

*Yield: ¼ cup*

## Turkey Club Wrap

This wrap can be made with chicken instead of turkey.

1 tbsp Basil Mayonnaise (above)
1 slice bacon, cooked crisp and crumbled
⅓ cup diced cooked turkey

I large leaf romaine lettuce
I 10-inch whole wheat soft flour tortilla
½ tomato, seeded and diced
¼ avocado, diced
I squeeze fresh lemon juice
I tsp light cream cheese

- The night before, prepare Basil Mayonnaise and cook bacon. In small bowl, combine Basil Mayonnaise, bacon and turkey, and refrigerate overnight.
- In the morning, place lettuce in centre of tortilla. Spread turkey mixture on lettuce in 8-inch vertical strip and top with tomatoes.
- Toss together avocado and lemon juice, and scatter over turkey mixture.
- Spread ½-inch strip of cream cheese along right-hand end of tortilla.
- Wrap lettuce around filling, then fold 1½-inch bottom end of tortilla toward centre, and roll up tightly from left toward cream cheese edge, pressing to seal. Place seam side down in reusable container.

*Yield: Serves 1*

## Veggie Hummus Wrap

Add a few drops of hot sauce to this wrap if your child likes a bit of heat.

3 tbsp Homemade Hummus (page 97) or your favourite store-bought equivalent
4 strips sweet red pepper
4 2-inch strips of cucumber, seeded and julienned
½ tomato, seeded and diced
½ large dill pickle, quartered

1 tsp finely diced red onion (optional)
1 carrot, grated
1 large leaf green leaf lettuce
1 10-inch whole wheat soft flour tortilla
½ tsp light cream cheese

- The night before, prepare Homemade Hummus if using. Cut red pepper, cucumber, tomato, pickle and onion (if using) and grate carrot. Refrigerate overnight.
- In the morning, place lettuce in centre of tortilla. Spread hummus in 8-inch strip in centre of lettuce. Top with red pepper, cucumber, carrot, tomato, pickle and onion (if using).
- Spread ½-inch strip of cream cheese along right-hand end of tortilla.
- Wrap lettuce around filling, then fold 1½-inch bottom end of tortilla toward centre, and roll up tightly from left toward cream cheese edge, pressing to seal. Place seam side down in reusable container.

*Yield: Serves 1*

## Charlie's Chicken Souvlaki Wrap

Named after Brenda's son, this wrap is Charlie's favourite sandwich. Some tzatziki on the side for dipping is always welcome.

1 rounded tbsp Minted Tzatziki (page 97) or store-bought equivalent
4 1-inch strips of cucumber, seeded
½ small tomato, seeded and diced
⅓ cup diced cooked chicken
1 large leaf green leaf lettuce
1 10-inch whole wheat soft flour tortilla
½ tsp light cream cheese

- The night before, prepare Minted Tzatziki if using. Cut up cucumber, tomato and chicken, and refrigerate overnight.
- In the morning, place lettuce in centre of tortilla. Evenly spread Minted Tzatziki in 8-inch vertical strip in centre of lettuce. Top with cucumber, tomatoes and chicken.
- Spread ½-inch strip of cream cheese along right-hand end of tortilla.
- Wrap lettuce around filling, then fold 1½-inch bottom end of tortilla toward centre, and roll up tightly from left toward cream cheese edge, pressing to seal. Place seam side down in reusable container.

*Yield: Serves 1*

## Packing Fibre

Fibre should be an important part of your child's lunch box. Since dietary fibre comes from plant sources and cannot be fully digested or absorbed, it helps prevent constipation by regulating bowel function. High fibre foods are more filling than lower fibre options, and they also tend to be lower in calories—so increasing fibre intake is one of the key principles in preventing obesity and maintaining a healthy weight.

In fact, a recent study looking at overweight children between the ages of 11 and 17 found that those who increased their fibre intake over a 2-year period had a 4 per cent drop in abdominal obesity, while those who consumed less fibre experienced a 21 per cent increase in belly fat. The study's authors believe that a modest increase in dietary fibre (equivalent to 1 whole wheat tortilla or ½ cup of beans per day) could have a significant impact on abdominal obesity.[21] This is an important finding because abdominal obesity is associated with an increased risk of both heart disease and diabetes.

To increase your child's intake of fibre, be sure to pack at least 2 servings of Vegetables and Fruit in their lunch box. Make salads with whole grains (quinoa, bulgur or brown rice) and add legumes to both salads and soups. Always make sandwiches, wraps and pita pockets with whole grain breads and buy whole grain products whenever possible. When buying these products, always look at the fibre content on the Nutrition Facts table and avoid relying on front package claims, which are often ambiguous. Just because bread is labelled "multi-grain," doesn't necessarily mean it is made with whole grain flour. "Multi-grain" merely means that a variety of grains were used.

## Grated Veggie Wrap

Packed full of fibre, this sandwich is sure to satisfy your ravenous teen.

| | |
|---|---|
| 1 tomato, seeded and diced | 1 large leaf romaine lettuce |
| 5 slices cucumber, seeded and diced | 1 10-inch whole wheat soft flour tortilla |
| 5 strips sweet red pepper | ¼ avocado |
| ¼ cup grated beet | 1 squeeze fresh lime juice |
| 2 tbsp grated carrot | 2 tbsp crumbled feta cheese |
| 2 tsp finely diced onion (optional) | 1 rounded tsp mustard |
| | 1 tsp cream cheese |

- The night before, chop or grate cucumber, red pepper, beet, carrot and onion (if using) and refrigerate overnight.
- In the morning, place lettuce in centre of tortilla.
- In small bowl, mash avocado with lime juice, and spread in 8-inch vertical strip in centre of lettuce. Top with cucumber, red pepper, beet, carrot and onion (if using). Evenly scatter feta cheese over vegetables.
- Evenly spread mustard along left-hand side of tortilla, and spread ½-inch strip of cream cheese along right-hand end of tortilla.
- Wrap lettuce around filling, then fold 1½-inch bottom end

of tortilla toward centre, and roll up tightly from left toward cream cheese edge, pressing to seal. Place seam side down in reusable container.

*Yield: Serves 1*

## Asian Chili Mayonnaise

¼ cup mayonnaise
½ tsp Sriracha Asian chili hot sauce, or more if preferred
½ tsp soy sauce
4 drops sesame oil

• In small bowl, combine ingredients thoroughly.

*Yield: ¼ cup*

## Asian Chili Chicken Wrap

This is also good with shrimp—just substitute an equal amount of shrimp for the chicken.

¹/₃ cup diced cooked chicken
1 large radish, diced
1 tbsp diced water chestnuts or celery
1 tsp finely chopped fresh cilantro (optional)
1 rounded tbsp Asian Chili Mayonnaise (above)
4 strips sweet red pepper
3 snow peas, trimmed and cut lengthwise into thin strips
1 large leaf green leaf lettuce
1 10-inch whole wheat soft flour tortilla
½ tsp light cream cheese

• The night before, in a small bowl, combine chicken,

Sandwiches

radishes, water chestnuts, cilantro and Asian Chili Mayonnaise. Slice red pepper and snow peas. Refrigerate overnight.

- In the morning, place lettuce in centre of tortilla. Top with chicken mixture, red pepper and snow peas.
- Spread ½-inch strip of cream cheese along right-hand end of tortilla.
- Wrap lettuce around filling, then fold 1½-inch bottom end of tortilla toward centre, and roll up tightly from left toward cream cheese edge, pressing to seal. Place seam side down in reusable container.

*Yield: Serves 1*

## Chicken Veggie Wrap

¹/₃ cup diced cooked chicken
¹/₃ stalk celery, diced
1 tbsp chopped fresh cilantro (optional)
1 tbsp mayonnaise
¼ carrot, julienned
¼ tomato, seeded and diced
¼ green onion, cut into thin strips (optional)
2 tbsp finely shredded cabbage (optional)
1 large leaf green leaf lettuce
1 10-inch whole wheat soft flour tortilla
½ tsp light cream cheese

- The night before, in small bowl, combine chicken, celery, cilantro (if using) and mayonnaise. Cut up carrot, tomato and green onion and shred cabbage (if using). Refrigerate overnight.
- In the morning, place lettuce in centre of wrap. Spread chicken mixture in 2-inch strip in centre of lettuce. Top

Sandwiches

with carrot, tomato, green onion and cabbage (if using).
- Spread ½-inch strip of cream cheese along right-hand end of tortilla.
- Wrap lettuce around filling, then fold 1½-inch bottom end of tortilla toward centre, and roll up tightly from left toward cream cheese edge, pressing to seal. Place seam side down in reusable container.

*Yield: Serves 1*

# Quesadillas

While quesadillas may seem like an odd choice for the lunch box, kids love them whether they are served hot or cold. This means they can be made and packed the night before. When making quesadillas for the lunch box, be sure to cook the tortilla until it's crispy and allow it to cool thoroughly by placing it on a wire rack before packing. This prevents condensation from forming inside the container. Quesadillas can be served with salsa or ketchup packed in a separate container for dipping.

## Pizza Quesadillas

If your children have simpler tastes, you can always omit the tomato paste in this recipe to make a plain cheese quesadilla.

1 rounded tbsp tomato paste
2 10-inch whole wheat soft flour tortillas
3 tbsp mozzarella cheese, shredded
3 tbsp Cheddar cheese, shredded

- The night before, evenly spread tomato paste over 1 tortilla and place it tortilla side down in large skillet.
- Evenly scatter cheeses over tortilla and top with remaining tortilla. Cook over medium heat for approximately 4 to 7

Sandwiches

minutes on each side or until cheese melts and tortilla is crispy and beginning to brown.

- Remove from skillet, place on wire rack and let cool completely. Cut quesadilla into triangles and pack in reusable container. Repeat with second tortilla. Refrigerate overnight.

*Yield: Serves 1 or 2 small children*

## Quesadilla with Chicken, Beans and Cheese

**2 tbsp refried beans**
**2 10-inch whole wheat soft flour tortillas**
**1/4 cup diced cooked chicken**
**1/4 cup shredded Cheddar cheese**

- The night before, evenly spread refried beans over 1 tortilla and place it tortilla side down in large skillet.
- Evenly scatter chicken and cheese over beans and top with remaining tortilla. Cook over medium heat for approximately 4 to 7 minutes on each side or until cheese melts and tortilla is crispy and beginning to brown.
- Remove from skillet, place on wire rack and let cool completely. Cut quesadilla into triangles and pack in reusable container. Repeat with second tortilla. Refrigerate overnight.

*Yield: Serves 1 or 2 small children*

Sandwiches

4.

Picnic-Style
Lunches
and Snacks

This chapter includes a variety of different snack options. Snacks can be packed as an accompaniment to sandwiches, salads and Thermoses of warm food. They can also be put together to make "picnic lunches." Picnic-style lunches contain a variety of appetizers or finger foods. These bite-sized morsels are quick to grab and easy to eat, which makes picnic lunches ideal for those who are in a rush to get to the playground.

When creating picnic lunches, try to include at least 1 food from each of the 4 food groups. For example, a healthy picnic may include a hard-boiled egg, whole grain rice crackers, veggies with dip, a few slices of cheese and 100% pure fruit juice. For many children, picnic lunches are a welcome change from sandwich lunches.

## The Greek Picnic

To make a Greek picnic, pack hummus and/or tzatziki with either whole wheat pita bread or Toasted Whole Wheat Pita Chips (page 88). For dipping, add a variety of fresh vegetables such as strips of sweet green, red and yellow peppers, slices of cucumber, and cherry tomatoes. To complete your picnic, pack a few chunks of feta cheese with some olives. If packing for younger children, look for pitted olives or remove the pits yourself. Spanakopita (page 87) also goes well with the Greek Picnic.

## The Ploughman's Lunch

Named after the classic British pub fare, the Ploughman's Lunch generally consists of bread, meat, cheese, pickles and sometimes a little salad. When packing a Ploughman's Lunch, be sure to include a few slices of Cheddar cheese or your child's favourite low-fat alternative with either whole wheat bread or good quality whole grain crackers such as Wasa, Finn Crisp or whole grain rice crackers. When buying crackers read and compare the Nutrition Facts tables to help you choose those that are high in fibre and low in sodium. Always pack cheese and crackers separately because the cheese will sweat, causing the crackers to go soggy. Add to the cheese and crackers a pickle, some brightly coloured veggie sticks and either a slice or a few cubes of whatever meat you have left over from last night's dinner. For occasional variety add a few slices of good quality turkey salami or even a turkey pepperoni stick.

# Middle Eastern Picnic

To assemble a Middle Eastern Picnic, pack 3 to 5 Lamb Meatballs (below) with tzatziki and/or hummus for dipping. Add to this a few triangles of whole wheat pita bread and some strips of sweet red pepper, cherry tomatoes, a few slices of cucumber, a chunk of feta cheese, a few olives, and a piece of fruit for dessert.

## Lamb Meatballs

These freeze well, are convenient to have on hand and can be used in a variety of different lunch options. They can be served as part of a Middle Eastern Picnic (above), in Lamb Meatball Souvlaki (page 66) or even in Italian Meatball Soup (page 119).

If you are not a fan of lamb, you can always substitute it with an equal portion of beef.

3 tbsp olive oil
1 onion, finely diced
1 shallot, finely diced
½ tsp kosher salt
Freshly ground pepper
½ cup Whole Wheat Bread Crumbs (page 86)
4 garlic cloves, minced
2 tsp ground cumin

1 tsp ground coriander
1½ lbs (24 oz/750 g) ground lamb
1 egg
½ cup chopped fresh parsley
¼ cup chopped fresh mint
2 tbsp tomato paste

Picnic-Style Lunches

- Preheat oven to 350°F.
- Heat oil in skillet over medium heat. Add onions, shallots, salt and pepper to taste, and sauté for 5 minutes.
- Add bread crumbs, garlic, cumin and coriander and continue to sauté for another 5 minutes. Remove from heat and let cool.
- In large bowl, combine lamb, egg, parsley, mint, tomato paste and onion mixture.
- Roll 1 tbsp lamb mixture to form ball. Place on unoiled

baking sheet; repeat with remaining lamb mixture. Bake until meatballs are cooked through, approximately 20 minutes. Transfer to kitchen towel to drain. Extra meatballs can be frozen in airtight containers.

*Yield: Approximately 45 meatballs*

## Whole Wheat Bread Crumbs

**4 slices whole wheat bread**

- Lightly toast bread. Remove from toaster and allow to stand for 5 minutes until bread is dry.
- Pulse in food processor until crumbs are fine consistency.

*Yield: Approximately 1 cup*

### Yogurt Pots

To avoid the additives, artificial colouring and high sugar content of many commercial yogurts, some of which contain as much as 3 to 4 tsp of sugar per serving, consider buying plain yogurt in bulk and making your own yogurt pots. Not only is this a healthier option, it also serves to reduce the waste associated with single use containers.

To make yogurt pots, invest in some small containers with tight-fitting lids. Place approximately $2/3$ cup of yogurt in a container and stir in $1/4$ cup of fresh fruit. The following combinations work well: diced fresh or frozen berries (raspberries, strawberries and blueberries), grated apple, diced mango, diced kiwi and a little mashed banana with some chopped up dates or raisins. A squeeze of lemon juice should prevent the banana from browning. Roasted Fruit (page 37) is also yummy with plain yogurt. If your children complain that the yogurt isn't sweet enough, you can always add a drizzle of honey or fruit-sweetened jam. And of course, a sprinkling of granola is always delicious with fruit and yogurt.

# Spanakopita

Loaded with spinach and feta cheese, these tasty snacks make a nutritious lunch box treat. Extra spanakopita can be frozen prior to baking. (If freezing spanakopita, place parchment paper between the layers of spanakopita so they don't stick together.) To get one ready for the lunch box, defrost it in the refrigerator overnight and bake it while the children eat their breakfast. Once baked, spanakopita are good for several days and make a delicious lunch when served with tzatziki for dipping.

Although butter is traditionally used to make spanakopita, we use non-hydrogenated margarine because, unlike butter, it is rich in heart healthy unsaturated fatty acids.

| | |
|---|---|
| 1 package (1 lb/454 g) phyllo pastry, thoroughly thawed outside of the package | 2 bunches green onion, thinly sliced |
| | 3 eggs, beaten |
| 1 ½ cups non-hydrogenated margarine, melted | 14 oz / 400 g feta cheese, crumbled |
| 12 cups packed chopped spinach | Juice of 1 lemon |
| | 2 tbsp olive oil |
| | ½ tsp freshly ground pepper |

- Preheat oven to 375°F.
- In small saucepan over low heat, melt margarine.
- In large bowl, combine spinach, onion, eggs, feta cheese, lemon juice, olive oil and pepper.
- Cut phyllo into 16-inch long rectangle and lay on clean surface. Depending on which brand of pastry you use, phyllo may already be cut for you. Cover remaining phyllo with ever so slightly damp tea towel so it doesn't dry out.
- Brush phyllo rectangle with melted margarine. Cut another rectangle, place on top of first one and brush with margarine again. Cut phyllo rectangle in half vertically, creating 2 strips. Place ⅓ cup spinach mixture at one end of phyllo strip. Fold one corner over other to enclose filling, creating triangle. Flip

triangle end over end until you come to end of phyllo strip. The result will be a layered triangle. Press edges with fingers to seal. Repeat with remaining spinach and phyllo. If phyllo seems a little dry, you may want to brush edges with melted margarine as you turn triangle end over end.

• Bake 15 to 20 minutes, or until golden brown.

*Yield: Approximately 2 dozen*

## Little Dippers

Kids love to dip their food, so try these healthy snacks and let them go to it!

Dip cherry tomatoes, baby carrots, mini cucumbers or slices of cucumber, and strips of sweet red, yellow or green peppers into low-fat ranch dressing, Minted Tzatziki (page 97) or Homemade Hummus (page 97).

Dip veggies and Toasted Whole Wheat Pita Chips (page 88), whole grain crackers or whole wheat pita bread into tzatziki, Homemade Hummus (page 97) or other bean dips.

Dip a granola bar or homemade cookie into low-fat yogurt.

Dip a good quality turkey sausage or tofu dog into ketchup, mustard or salsa.

Dip baked tortilla chips into Homemade Hummus (page 97), other bean dips or salsa.

Dip graham crackers into low-fat yogurt or Strawberry Applesauce (page 37).

Dip fruit such as strawberries, cherries, cubes of cantaloupe or papaya, and apple slices into low-fat yogurt.

## Toasted Whole Wheat Pita Chips

This recipe comes from our family food cookbook *The Good Food Book for Families* and is a healthy alternative to store-bought crackers. The recipe makes a fairly large quantity of pita chips. Extra chips can be stored in an airtight container for up to 10 days.

4 whole wheat pitas
¼ cup olive oil
1 garlic clove, minced
½ tsp kosher salt
¼ tsp freshly ground pepper

- Preheat oven to 425°F.
- Heat pitas in microwave for 30 seconds. When warmed, pita pockets will open with ease. Slit top of pita pocket with knife and separate 2 sides of pita. Repeat with remaining pitas. Cut each half of pita into quarters and place on unoiled baking sheet.
- In small bowl, combine olive oil, garlic, salt and pepper. With pastry brush, brush oil mixture over each pita triangle.
- Bake until chips are golden and beginning to brown around edges, approximately 5 minutes.

*Yield: 32 chips*

### Snacks to Pack

- Dried fruit and toasted sunflower seeds and/or pumpkin seeds with a few dark chocolate chips—or just the seeds themselves
- Air-popped popcorn, plain or sprinkled with melted non-hydrogenated margarine and a little grated Parmesan cheese
- Raisins on their own or combined with other dried fruit and seeds
- Assorted olives
- Sesame snaps and good quality granola bars
- Hard-boiled eggs (shell removed for young children)
- Baked corn chips with a mixture of salsa, black beans and shredded cheese for dipping
- A small container of your child's favourite whole grain cereal, plain or combined with diced dried fruit or blueberries.

Picnic-Style
Lunches

- Yogurt Pots (page 86)
- Peanuts or other nuts if permitted by your school
- Vegetable chips made from carrots, beets and sweet potatoes
- Yogurt-covered raisins
- Fruit-Filled Jell-O Fingers (page 39)

## Devilled Eggs

Make sure your children like smoked paprika before sprinkling it on these eggs. Smoked paprika has a fairly distinct flavour.

I hard-boiled egg
I tbsp finely diced celery
Approximately I tsp mayonnaise
Pinch of smoked paprika

- Cut egg in half, scoop out egg yolk and place in small bowl, leaving egg whites intact.
- Add celery and mayonnaise to egg yolk and combine. Spoon into egg whites and sprinkle lightly with smoked paprika.

*Yield: Serves 1*

### The Sunshine Vitamin

Vitamin D, sometimes referred to as the sunshine vitamin, is, in fact, a group of hormones obtained from sun exposure, food and dietary supplements. It has long been known that vitamin D plays a crucial role in maintaining healthy bones and teeth, but over the past few years there has been increasing evidence to suggest vitamin D plays a significant role in the prevention of a variety of diseases, including cancer, multiple sclerosis, rheumatoid arthritis, inflammatory bowel disease and diabetes.

As a result, it is extremely important that children, as well as adults, get enough vitamin D. The vitamin is readily made by the body upon exposure to sunlight, but because Canada is so far north, it can be difficult to get enough the old-fashioned way. In addition to our latitudinal disadvantage is the fact that children spend an increasing amount of time indoors and when outside may be almost entirely covered up with clothing and sunscreen. Children with darker skin tones are at an even higher risk for vitamin D deficiency. In fact, a study done in Edmonton found that 34 per cent of children ages 2 to 12 had insufficient vitamin D levels.[22]

Given the mounting evidence, the US and Canadian governments commissioned a joint review of the Dietary Reference Intakes for vitamin D and, as a result, new recommendations have been established. The recommended dietary allowance (RDA) for Canadians 1 to 70 years old has been set at 600 IU (international units) per day. The tolerable upper intake level of vitamin D, that is, the amount that is likely to pose no risk of adverse health effects, has been set at 2,500 IU for children 1 to 3 years of age, 3,000 IU for children 4 to 8 years of age and 4,000 IU for all Canadians over the age of 9.[23] If you are considering supplementing your children with vitamin D, talk to your doctor about dosage.

Regardless of whether you decide to supplement your children or not, it's important that you make an effort to serve a variety of foods containing vitamin D. These foods include cow's milk, fortified soy beverages, non-hydrogenated margarine, eggs, liver and fatty fish such as mackerel, tuna, sardines and salmon. To get the maximum amount of vitamin D, choose wild salmon over farmed, since farmed salmon contains approximately a quarter of the vitamin D content that wild does.[24] For more information on farmed salmon, see page 129.

## Mini Flourless Quiches

Because there is no pastry to deal with, these quiches are a snap to make. They can be baked the night before and refrigerated overnight, or you can prepare them the night before and bake them in the morning. They can be eaten on their own or served with ketchup or salsa for dipping. They also make an easy last-minute breakfast. Extra quiches freeze well; to serve, defrost, heat and eat.

## Tomato, Basil and Feta Cheese Quiche

I egg, beaten
I cherry tomato, sliced

I tsp finely chopped basil
I tbsp crumbled feta cheese

- Preheat oven to 350°F. Grease 1 muffin tin cup with either non-hydrogenated margarine or canola oil. Fill remaining cups with water.
- In small bowl, combine egg, cherry tomato, basil and feta cheese. Pour into greased muffin cup.
- Bake for 20 minutes or until quiche is puffed and egg is set. Transfer muffin tin to wire rack to cool for 5 minutes. With a knife, gently loosen edges of quiche and remove from pan.

*Yield: Serves 1*

## Cheddar Cheese and Broccoli Quiche

I egg, beaten
I floret broccoli, cooked tender-crisp and chopped
I tbsp shredded Cheddar cheese

- Preheat oven to 350°F. Grease 1 muffin tin cup with either non-hydrogenated margarine or canola oil. Fill remaining cups with water.
- In small bowl, combine egg, broccoli and cheese. Pour into greased muffin cup.
- Bake for 20 minutes or until quiche is puffed and egg is set. Transfer muffin tin to wire rack to cool for 5 minutes. With knife, gently loosen edges of quiche and remove from pan.

*Yield: Serves 1*

## Bacon, Pea and Cheese Quiche

1 egg, beaten
1 tbsp cooked bacon, crumbled
1 tbsp frozen peas, thawed
1 tbsp shredded Cheddar cheese

- Preheat oven to 350°F. Grease 1 muffin tin cup with either non-hydrogenated margarine or canola oil. Fill remaining cups with water.
- In small bowl, combine egg, bacon, peas and cheese. Pour into greased muffin cup.
- Bake for 20 minutes or until quiche is puffed and egg is set. Transfer muffin tin to wire rack to cool for 5 minutes. With knife, gently loosen edges of quiche and remove from pan.

*Yield: Serves 1*

## Mini Salmon Patties

These are a wonderful lunch box snack. They are exceptionally versatile and freeze well. They can be placed on a salad, wrapped in a pita pocket (page 67) or served on their own with a little tzatziki for dipping. Try doubling the recipe and freezing the extras so you have plenty on hand.

2 tbsp canola oil
1/2 cup diced onion
1/2 stalk celery, diced
1 garlic clove, minced (optional)
2 cans (7 1/2 oz/213 g each) salmon, drained and skin removed
2 large eggs, beaten
1/2 cup Whole Wheat Bread Crumbs (page 86)
1 squeeze fresh lemon juice
1/2 rounded tsp chopped fresh dill (optional)
1/2 tsp freshly ground pepper
1/4 tsp lemon zest

- Heat 1 tbsp of oil in skillet over medium heat. Add onions and celery and sauté for 8 minutes.
- Add garlic (if using) and sauté for another 2 minutes, being careful not to burn garlic.
- In bowl, combine onion mixture, salmon, eggs, bread crumbs, lemon juice, dill, pepper and lemon zest.
- Shape 2 tbsp salmon mixture into patty. Repeat with remaining salmon mixture.
- Heat remaining 1 tbsp of oil in skillet, and cook patties for 4 to 6 minutes per side or until golden brown with slightly crispy coating.

*Yield: Approximately 12 salmon patties*

### Recess!

Be sure to pack a separate snack for recess that can be eaten on the go. Active, growing kids need to eat every 2 to 3 hours to keep their blood sugar levels stable. Portable snack ideas include a piece of fruit, veggie sticks and your healthy, homemade baked goods (muffins, granola bars, etc.).

## Nanny Di's Bits and Bites

Traditionally bits and bites are made with nuts rather than seeds, as they are in this recipe. If you prefer them with nuts, substitute equal amounts of peanuts for the sunflower seeds and mixed nuts for the pumpkin seeds.

8 cups (approximately 1 small box Cheerios)
8 cups (approximately 1 small box Shreddies)
5 cups pretzels
3 cups raw sunflower seeds
1 cup roasted pumpkin seeds
3/4 cup non-hydrogenated margarine

3 to 5 garlic cloves (depending on personal preference), minced

2 tbsp Worcestershire sauce

- Preheat oven to 250°F.
- In large roasting pan with lid, combine cereal, pretzels and seeds.
- Melt margarine in small saucepan over medium heat. Add garlic and Worcestershire sauce and combine. Pour over cereal mixture, stirring as you pour. Cover roasting pan with lid and thoroughly shake to disperse margarine mixture.
- Remove lid and bake for 2 hours, stirring every 15 minutes.

*Yield: 25 cups*

## Nut-free Trail Mix

The chocolate chips in this recipe are optional, although they do go a long way in getting little ones to gobble up this nutritious snack. If your school permits nuts, you can add 1 cup of peanuts to the mix.

1 cup toasted sunflower seeds
½ cup toasted pumpkin seeds
½ cup raisins
½ cup dried cranberries
½ cup chocolate chips (optional)

- In bowl, combine ingredients. Store in airtight container.

*Yield: 3 cups*

Picnic-Style Lunches

## When "Kid-friendly" Foods Are Anything But

A recent study analyzing the nutritional content of food products marketed for and to children found that 89 per cent of these foods could be classified as poor in terms of nutritional quality. This was due to high levels of fat, sugar and sodium. The study focused on regular food items such as dry goods, dairy products and refrigerated and frozen foods—many of which are specifically marketed for children's lunch boxes—and excluded obvious junk food such as candy, soft drinks, potato chips, etc. More alarming, despite the poor nutritional quality of these foods, 63 per cent of them made one or more nutritional claims on the front of the package that were designed to entice health-conscious parents into buying them.[25]

We need to move away from the idea that children need special food just for them. Too often these so-called "kid foods" are low in quality, and they can contribute to kids developing a preference for the flavour of highly processed foods. If this habit is continued throughout their lifespan, it can lead to a myriad of health consequences, including obesity, diabetes, cardiovascular disease and cancer. Instead, children should be eating regular meals with the rest of the family and following similar nutritional guidelines. This means eating a wide variety of fruit and vegetables, whole grains, low-fat dairy products and lean sources of protein such as fish, poultry, lean cuts of red meat and legumes.

## Dips

Served with Toasted Whole Wheat Pita Chips (page 88) or vegetable sticks, dips are the perfect accompaniment to any lunch and, of course, the ideal way to entice kids to eat their veggies. The following dips are healthy alternatives to store-bought varieties, which tend to be high in fat, sodium and chemical preservatives.

## Minted Tzatziki

This recipe can also be made with dill. To make Dilled Tzatziki, substitute an equal amount of dill for the mint.

2 cups plain Greek-style yogurt
(or any plain yogurt above 3% milk fat)
½ English cucumber, grated
3 tbsp finely chopped fresh mint
2 to 3 garlic cloves, minced
Kosher salt and freshly ground pepper

- Place yogurt in fine-mesh sieve suspended over bowl for 5 minutes to remove excess liquid.
- Squeeze cucumber to remove excess liquid. Transfer to small bowl, and mix in mint, 2 garlic cloves and salt and pepper to taste. Refrigerate for 30 minutes.
- Taste and add another minced garlic clove if needed.

*Yield: 3 cups*

## Homemade Hummus

1 can (540mL/19oz) chickpeas, rinsed and drained, reserving ½ cup of the liquid
¼ cup fresh lemon juice

¼ cup tahini
2 to 3 garlic cloves, minced
1 tsp ground cumin
Drizzle of extra-virgin olive oil

- In bowl of food processor, place chickpeas, chickpea liquid, lemon juice, tahini, 2 garlic cloves and cumin, and process until smooth. Refrigerate for 30 minutes.
- Taste and add another minced garlic clove if needed. To serve, drizzle with olive oil.

*Yield: 2 cups*

# Roasted Red Pepper and Basil Hummus

This hummus can also be made without basil. However, the basil does look pretty and adds a delicious flavour.

1 sweet red pepper, cut in half and seeded
1 can (540mL/19oz) chickpeas, rinsed and drained
6 tbsp extra-virgin olive oil
1/3 cup plain Greek-style yogurt
(or any plain yogurt above 3% milk fat)
1 to 2 garlic cloves, minced
1/4 tsp kosher salt
1 tbsp finely sliced fresh basil

- To roast pepper: Place red pepper halves cut-side down on baking sheet lined with foil; broil in oven 10 to 15 minutes, or until skin begins to bubble and blacken. Remove from oven, wrap in foil and allow to sit for 20 minutes. Peel skin.
- In bowl of food processor or using hand-held immersion blender, process red pepper, chickpeas, 1/4 cup extra-virgin olive oil, yogurt, 1 garlic clove and salt until smooth. Refrigerate for 20 minutes.
- Taste and add another minced garlic clove if needed. To serve, sprinkle with basil and drizzle with remaining 2 tbsp olive oil.

*Yield: 2½ cups*

Picnic-Style Lunches

## Dilly Delicious Dip

To make a lighter version of this dip, use low-fat mayonnaise.

1/2 cup mayonnaise
1/2 cup low-fat plain yogurt
2 tbsp plus I tsp finely chopped fresh dill
Kosher salt and freshly ground pepper

• In small bowl, combine mayonnaise, yogurt and dill. Add salt and pepper to taste and refrigerate for at least 1 hour before serving.

*Yield: 1 cup*

5.

Soups

On a winter's day, there is nothing better than homemade soup to warm a hungry tummy. Packed full of vegetables, the following soups are wholesome, nutritious and versatile. Most are designed to be made in bulk and frozen in individual containers for easy, last-minute lunches. In the morning, simply reheat and pour into a preheated Thermos.

Accompanied by some whole grain bread, a chunk of cheese and a piece of fruit or yogurt for dessert, homemade soup is a nutritious lunch your children are sure to love. The puréed texture of many of the homemade soups in this chapter is the perfect way to disguise vegetables for those who are reluctant to eat them. If your child rejects a soup because she spots some vegetables floating in it, try puréeing it another day.

Adding legumes such as chickpeas, lentils, navy beans, black beans, peas and kidney beans to soups is a good way to increase your child's intake of protein and cholesterol-lowering fibre. In addition to being packed full of vitamins and minerals, legumes are high in fibre and take longer to break down. This means that they supply a steady stream of slow-release energy that will keep your children going all afternoon. Any of the recipes in this book that call for legumes can be made with either canned beans or dried beans that have been soaked and cooked (see page 105 for cooking instructions).

The majority of the following soups do not contain meat. However, they do call for chicken stock. If you prefer to keep the soups strictly vegetarian, simply substitute vegetable stock for the chicken stock.

## Homemade Salt-Free Chicken Stock

Making your own chicken stock is a great way to avoid the high sodium content of most commercial stocks. If you don't have a chicken carcass on hand, don't let this stop you from making homemade chicken stock. You can buy inexpensive chicken necks, backs and wing tips from most butchers. If you are in a pinch and don't have time to make homemade stock, look for salt-free or low-sodium broth at your local grocery store. Be aware that if a broth is labelled "25% less sodium," it doesn't necessarily mean that it is low in sodium. In fact, many of these broths are still very high in sodium. For a product to be low in sodium, it has to have a percentage daily value (% DV) of sodium that is 5% or less. A product that is high in sodium will have a percentage daily value of sodium that is 15% or more. If using commercial broth, always taste the soup before adding salt. If the soup contains lots of spices and herbs, it is likely you won't need to add any salt at all.

| | |
|---|---|
| 1 chicken carcass | 1 tomato, quartered |
| 1 chicken neck and giblets (if available) | 2 dried bay leaves |
| | 1 sprig fresh thyme |
| 1 onion, quartered | 1 sprig fresh tarragon |
| 5 large carrots, cut into chunks | 10 peppercorns |
| | 1 garlic clove |
| 4 stalks celery, cut into chunks | 12 cups cold water |

- Remove any good-quality meat from chicken carcass. Place carcass, neck and giblets (if available), onion, carrots, celery, tomatoes, bay leaves, thyme, tarragon, peppercorns and garlic in large stockpot. Cover with cold water and bring to boil. Reduce heat to low, and simmer for 3 hours. Remove from heat and let cool.
- Strain stock through fine sieve. Discard vegetables and carcass. Refrigerate until fat congeals on surface. Discard solidified fat.

*Yield: Approximately 8 cups*

Soups

# Lovely Lentil Soup

The addition of a few crushed red-pepper flakes gives this soup a mildly spicy flavour that is likely to appeal to most children. However, if your kids are particularly sensitive to spicy food, you may choose to omit the red-pepper flakes. You can always sprinkle them on the adults' portions prior to serving.

This soup can be served as is or puréed smooth, but we recommend using a hand-held immersion blender to partially purée the soup. This gives it a lovely, slightly lumpy texture.

2 tbsp canola oil
1 large onion, finely diced
2 large carrots, grated
10 garlic cloves, minced
1 tbsp freshly grated
  ginger
1 tbsp finely chopped
  fresh mint
¼ tsp crushed red-pepper
  flakes

2 cups red lentils, rinsed
  and picked over
8 to 9 cups Homemade
  Salt-Free Chicken Stock
  (page 102), or salt-free or
  low-sodium chicken broth
1 bunch fresh cilantro,
  chopped
Kosher salt and freshly
  ground pepper

- Heat oil in stockpot over medium heat. Add onion and sauté until softened, approximately 5 minutes.
- Add carrots, garlic, ginger, mint and red-pepper flakes, and continue to sauté for another 10 minutes, being careful not to burn the garlic.
- Add lentils and 8 cups of chicken stock and bring to rapid boil. Reduce heat and simmer, partially covered, for approximately 40 minutes or until lentils are tender.
- Remove from heat. Using hand-held immersion blender, partially purée soup so that it still has slightly lumpy texture.
- Add cilantro and salt and pepper to taste. If soup seems too thick, add more stock as desired.

*Yield: 12 cups*

## Instructions for Cooking Dried Beans

Dried beans can be used instead of canned beans in any of the recipes. They are less expensive and have a nice firm texture. Before dried legumes (with the exception of split peas and lentils) can be used in a recipe, they need to be soaked in 3 to 4 times their volume of water for 8 hours or overnight. Once soaked, they should be cooked in unsalted water. Place beans in a saucepan and cover with cold water. Bring to a boil and gently simmer until tender. See chart below for approximate simmering times.

| SOAKED BEANS | SIMMERING TIME |
|---|---|
| Kidney beans | 40 to 50 minutes |
| Black beans | 40 to 45 minutes |
| Chickpeas | 80 to 85 minutes |
| Navy beans | 40 to 50 minutes |
| Great Northern beans | 40 to 50 minutes |

## Roasted Carrot Ginger Soup with Chickpeas

3½ lbs / 1.75 kg carrots, cut into 2½-inch chunks
9 tbsp canola oil, plus an extra drizzle
1 head garlic, topped
1 large onion, diced
⅓ cup freshly grated ginger
8 to 10 cups Homemade Salt-Free Chicken Stock (page 102), or salt-free or low-sodium chicken broth
1 can (19 oz/540 mL) chickpeas, drained and rinsed, or 2 cups cooked chickpeas
⅓ cup chopped fresh cilantro or parsley (optional)
Kosher salt and freshly ground pepper

- Preheat oven to 375°F. Line baking sheet with foil or parchment paper.
- Place carrots on baking sheet and drizzle with ⅓ cup oil. Toss to coat. Drizzle a little more oil on garlic, wrap with

foil and place on baking sheet. Bake for 45 minutes.

- Heat remaining ¼ cup oil in large stockpot over medium heat. Add onion and ginger and sauté until softened, approximately 10 to 12 minutes.
- Remove carrots and garlic from oven. Unwrap garlic and let cool.
- Squeeze garlic onto carrots and discard skin. Scrape roasted carrots, garlic and juices into stockpot. Using hand-held immersion blender, purée vegetables until smooth. (If you do not have hand blender, remove vegetables from pot and purée in food processor or blender.)
- Add 8 cups chicken stock and chickpeas and stir thoroughly. Bring to boil. Reduce heat and simmer with lid partially on for 20 minutes.
- Remove from heat and add cilantro (if using) and salt and pepper to taste. If soup seems too thick, add extra stock as desired.

*Yield: 12 cups*

## Roasted Winter Vegetable Soup

1 butternut squash (approximately 2 lbs or 1 kg), peeled, seeded and cut into 1-inch chunks

3 carrots, cut into 1½-inch chunks

3 parsnips, cut into 1½-inch chunks

1 leek, halved lengthwise and cut into 4-inch pieces

½ cup canola oil, plus an extra drizzle

1 head garlic, topped

5 tomatoes, quartered

1 onion, diced

2 tbsp ground cumin

1½ tbsp medium curry powder

8 to 10 cups Homemade Salt-Free Chicken Stock (page 102),

or salt-free or low-sodium chicken broth
½ cup chopped fresh parsley (optional)
Kosher salt and freshly ground pepper

- Preheat oven to 375°F.
- In roasting pan, toss squash, carrots, parsnips and leeks in ⅓ cup of oil until coated. Drizzle a little more oil over garlic, wrap in foil and place in roasting pan.
- In smaller roasting pan, toss tomatoes with 2 tbsp oil. Place both roasting pans in oven and roast for approximately 50 minutes, or until vegetables are tender.
- Heat remaining 1 tbsp oil in large stockpot over medium heat. Add onions and sauté until softened, approximately 5 to 7 minutes.
- Remove vegetables from oven and unwrap garlic. Let cool.
- Squeeze garlic into stockpot and discard skin. Add rest of roasted vegetables and their juices to stockpot, along with cumin and curry powder, and sauté for 5 minutes.
- Using hand-held immersion blender, purée vegetables until smooth. Add 8 cups of chicken stock, stir thoroughly and bring to boil. Reduce heat and simmer with lid partially on for 20 minutes.
- Remove from heat and add parsley (if using) and salt and pepper to taste. If soup seems too thick, add extra stock as desired.

*Yield: Approximately 12 cups*

Soups

Soups

## Save Exploring for Home

Avoid sending your child to school with new or unfamiliar foods. There is nothing more off-putting to young children than a large portion of unfamiliar food. New foods should be introduced at family meals so your children can see you enjoying them. Children are more likely to try new foods when they see others eating them.

It may take as many as 10 to 20 exposures to a new food before a young child will accept it. Don't assume your child dislikes fish because she rejected it once or even a few times. Instead, continue to offer it as part of your regular meal plan and be reassured that with each exposure, the chance of acceptance increases.

## Curried Chickpea and Vegetable Soup

3 tbsp canola oil
1 onion, diced
2 cans (19 oz/540 mL each) chickpeas, drained and rinsed, or 4 cups cooked chickpeas
3 garlic cloves, minced
1 ½ tbsp medium curry powder
1 tbsp ground cumin
2 tsp ground coriander
½ tsp ground turmeric
8 to 9 cups Homemade Salt-Free Chicken Stock (page 102), or salt-free or low-sodium chicken broth
1 cup chopped Swiss chard or kale
2 carrots, sliced
¾ cup chopped broccoli
¾ cup frozen peas
½ cup chopped fresh cilantro
Kosher salt and freshly ground pepper

- Heat oil in large stockpot over medium heat. Add onions and sauté for approximately 5 minutes, or until onions are softened.
- Add chickpeas, garlic, curry powder, cumin, coriander and turmeric and sauté for another 5 minutes.
- Add 8 cups of chicken stock and bring to boil. Reduce heat and simmer with lid partially on for 20 minutes.

- Using hand-held immersion blender, purée soup to fine consistency. Add Swiss chard, carrots and broccoli and continue to simmer for approximately 15 minutes, or until vegetables are tender. Add peas and simmer for another 5 minutes.
- Remove from heat and add cilantro and salt and pepper to taste.

*Yield: Approximately 10 to 12 cups*

## Shaking the Salt Habit

Sodium is found naturally in most foods—it's needed for cells to function properly and to regulate blood pressure. But sodium is also a major component of table salt, and the vast majority of Canadians, including children, consume far too much of it. In fact 93 per cent of children ages 4 to 8 consume more than the "tolerable upper limit."[26] Consumption exceeding this limit is thought to carry a risk of adverse health effects.

High salt intake has been linked to hypertension (or high blood pressure), which is the leading cause of death. In fact, hypertension increases your risk of heart attack, heart failure, stroke, dementia and kidney disease. It is estimated that hypertension accounts for more visits to the doctor than any other ailment.

The problem is that 77 per cent of the salt we consume comes from processed foods—salt that has been added to our food before we even open the package. Twelve per cent occurs naturally in foods, while 11 per cent is added during cooking or at the table.[26] Therefore the easiest way to avoid foods high in sodium is to eat a diet rich in whole foods and limit processed foods as much as possible. This isn't always as easy as it sounds—many foods that appear healthy are actually high in salt. This includes canned tomatoes, canned beans, canned vegetables, breakfast cereals, canned soups, canned chicken broth, etc. When buying these products, look for salt-free or low-sodium options and always rinse the salt off canned beans and vegetables. Keep salty foods out of the lunch box and don't encourage your children to develop a preference for them.

Soups

# Beef Barley Soup

When making this soup, choose pot barley over pearl barley. It has been through less refining and is, therefore, higher in fibre.

| | |
|---|---|
| 1 lb (500 g) stewing beef, visible fat removed | 1 can (14 oz/398 mL) diced tomatoes |
| 1 tbsp canola oil | ⅓ cup pot barley, rinsed |
| 1 large onion, diced | 3 dried bay leaves |
| 2 stalks celery, diced | 1 tsp dried oregano |
| 4 carrots, diced | 1 tsp dried thyme |
| 1 sweet red pepper, seeded and diced | 1 tsp chili powder |
| ¼ cup tomato paste | ⅓ cup chopped fresh parsley |
| 3 garlic cloves, minced | Kosher salt and freshly ground pepper |
| 8 to 10 cups salt-free or low-sodium beef broth | |

- Cut beef into small, bite-sized cubes. Heat oil in large stockpot over medium heat. Add beef and cook for 5 minutes, or until browned.
- Add onions, celery, carrots and red pepper, and sauté for another 8 minutes, or until vegetables are soft.
- Add tomato paste and garlic, and sauté for another 2 minutes. Add 8 cups beef broth, tomatoes, barley, bay leaves, oregano, thyme and chili powder, and bring to boil. Reduce heat and simmer with lid partially on for approximately 45 minutes, or until barley is tender.
- Remove from heat and add parsley and salt and pepper to taste. Remove bay leaves. If soup seems too thick, add extra stock as desired.

*Yield: Approximately 12 cups*

## Understanding Percentage Daily Values (% DV)

Percentage Daily Values (% DV) are listed on the Nutrition Facts tables of packaged foods. They are designed to help Canadians make informed decisions by giving the nutrient profiles of various foods. The % DV can be used to compare food products, helping Canadians choose the products that are higher in the nutrients they want to eat more of and lower in the nutrients they want to eat less of. If a nutrient has a % DV of 5 per cent or less, the food is generally considered low in that nutrient. If the % DV is 15 per cent or more, the food is considered high in that nutrient. The nutrients that most Canadians should be eating more of include calcium, iron, fibre, vitamin A, vitamin D and vitamin C. The nutrients many of us should be eating less of include fat, sugar, saturated and trans fats and sodium.

## Chickpea Soup

With or without cheese, this simple soup is a favourite of young children.

Soups

¼ cup canola oil
2½ cups packed finely sliced leeks
2 cans (19 oz/540 mL each) chickpeas, drained and rinsed, or 4 cups cooked chickpeas
4 garlic cloves, minced
7 cups Homemade Salt-Free Chicken Stock (page 102), or salt-free or low-sodium chicken broth
Kosher salt and freshly ground pepper
½ cup chopped fresh parsley
Shredded Cheddar cheese (optional)

- Heat oil in large stockpot over medium heat. Add leeks and sauté for 10 minutes.
- Add chickpeas and garlic and sauté for another 2 minutes. Add chicken stock and bring to rapid boil. Reduce heat and simmer with lid partially on for 25 minutes.

- Remove from heat. With slotted spoon, remove 1 cup of chickpeas and set aside. Using hand-held immersion blender, purée soup until smooth.
- Return chickpeas to stockpot and add salt and pepper to taste. Sprinkle with parsley.
- To serve, ladle into bowls or Thermoses, topping each serving with 1/3 cup shredded Cheddar cheese (if using). Stir until cheese melts.

*Yield: Approximately 12 cups*

**TIP:** The best way to keep soup hot is to pour it into a preheated Thermos: pour boiling water into the Thermos, put the lid on and let it stand for 5 minutes. Then pour the water out and put hot soup in.

## Mexican Black Bean Soup with Chicken

To make this soup vegetarian, simply omit the chicken and substitute vegetable stock for the chicken stock.

2 tbsp canola oil
1 onion, diced
2 carrots, diced
1 sweet red pepper, seeded and diced
1 can (14 oz/398 mL) diced tomatoes
1 cup canned black beans, drained and rinsed, or 1 cup cooked black beans
1 cup diced chicken
1 cup frozen corn

2 tbsp chili powder
1 tbsp ground cumin
1 tsp ground coriander
8 to 9 cups Homemade Salt-Free Chicken Stock (page 102), or salt-free or low-sodium chicken broth
1 cup chopped fresh cilantro
Kosher salt and freshly ground pepper

- Heat oil in large stockpot over medium heat. Add onion

and sauté for 5 minutes.
- Add carrots and red peppers and continue to sauté for 5 minutes.
- Add tomatoes, black beans, chicken, corn, chili powder, cumin and coriander and sauté for another 5 minutes.
- Add 8 cups chicken stock and stir thoroughly. Bring to rapid boil. Reduce heat and simmer with lid partially on for 30 minutes.
- Remove from heat. Add cilantro and salt and pepper to taste. If soup seems too thick, add extra stock as desired.

*Yield: 10 to 12 cups*

## Packing for Your Picky Eater

Young children and those with small appetites are easily overwhelmed by large portions. For these kids smaller servings work best. Instead of a whole sandwich, send half a sandwich cut into squares or triangles. Rather than a whole apple, send a few slices with a small piece of cheese. Your picky eater will feel less intimidated by a number of smaller servings.

Packing smaller portions is particularly important for children who are heading to school for the first time. The lunchroom is a busy place and young children are easily distracted. How can they focus on eating when there is so much to see? As disappointing as it may be to find an uneaten lunch, be reassured that this is quite normal and that your child's appetite will likely increase as the year progresses. In the meantime, keep portions small and make an effort to serve nutritious after-school snacks. If your child is going straight to an after-school activity, pack a snack that can be eaten en route. For tips on creating healthy snacks see Chapter 4.

Soups

# Chicken Lentil Mulligatawny

2 tbsp canola oil
1 onion, diced
3 or 4 carrots, diced
2 stalks celery, sliced
½ cup diced apple
1 or 2 garlic cloves, minced
1½ tsp medium curry
  powder
1 tsp ground cumin
½ tsp ground coriander
½ tsp ground turmeric
¼ tsp cayenne pepper
1 cup brown lentils

8 to 9 cups Homemade
  Salt-Free Chicken Stock
  (page 102), or salt-free or
  low-sodium chicken
  broth
1½ cups diced cooked
  chicken
1 can (14 oz/398 mL) light
  coconut milk
2 tbsp fresh lime juice
1 cup chopped fresh
  cilantro
Kosher salt and freshly
  ground pepper

- Heat oil in large stockpot over medium heat. Add onions and sauté for 5 minutes.
- Add carrots, celery, apple, garlic, curry powder, cumin, coriander, turmeric and cayenne pepper and continue to sauté for 10 minutes, stirring occasionally.
- Add lentils and stir until combined. Add 8 cups of chicken stock and bring to a boil. Reduce heat and add chicken, coconut milk and lime juice. Simmer with lid partially on for approximately 60 minutes, or until lentils are tender.
- Remove from heat. Add cilantro and salt and pepper to taste. If soup seems too thick, add extra stock as desired.

*Yield: Approximately 12 cups*

## Drink Milk and Stay Lean!

A study looking at adolescents (ages 12 to 16) found that lower dairy intake is associated with higher body fat.[27] Adding to this problem is the tendency for milk consumption to decline and soda pop consumption to rise during the teenage years. This trend is thought to be contributing to the childhood obesity epidemic.

Help your children stay lean and healthy by keeping high-calorie drinks (soda pop, fruit cocktails, energy drinks, fancy coffees, vitamin water, iced tea, etc.) out of the house. Aim to include at least 1 serving of Milk and Alternatives in their lunch box. To do so, add cheese to sandwiches and salads. Milk, fortified soy beverages or even Broccoli and Cheddar Cheese Soup (page 117) can be packed in a Thermos, and yogurt with fruit is the perfect accompaniment to any lunch. Remember that Health Canada's Food Guide recommends reading Nutrition Facts tables to help you choose lower fat dairy products.

## Roasted Tomato Lentil Soup

This soup is best enjoyed when tomatoes are in season—late summer or early fall—and therefore at their most flavourful. If you prefer, just omit the lentils for a roasted tomato soup.

| | |
|---|---|
| 4 lbs (2 kg) Roma tomatoes, quartered | 7 to 8 cups Homemade Salt-Free Chicken Stock (page 102), or salt-free or low-sodium chicken broth |
| ½ cup canola oil | |
| ½ tsp kosher salt | |
| 1 head garlic, topped | |
| 1 onion, diced | ¾ cup brown lentils |
| 2 large carrots, grated | 1 cup chopped fresh basil |
| ¼ cup tomato paste | Freshly ground pepper |

- Preheat oven to 375°F. Line baking sheet with foil or parchment paper.
- Place tomatoes on baking sheet and drizzle with ⅓ cup of oil. Sprinkle tomatoes with salt. Drizzle a little oil over

garlic, wrap in foil and place on baking sheet. Roast tomatoes and garlic for 45 minutes.

- Heat remaining 2 tbsp oil in stockpot over medium heat. Add onions and carrots and sauté for 10 minutes.
- Remove tomatoes and garlic from oven and unwrap garlic. Let cool.
- Squeeze garlic into stockpot and add tomatoes and their juices and tomato paste. Sauté for another 5 minutes to blend flavours.
- Using hand-held immersion blender, purée vegetables until smooth. Add 7 cups of stock, and stir thoroughly. Bring to boil, and add lentils. Turn heat down and simmer with lid partially on for approximately 50 minutes, or until lentils are tender.
- Remove from heat and add basil and pepper to taste. If soup seems too thick, add extra stock as desired.

*Yield: 10 cups*

## Chicken Noodle Soup

Any type of pasta or noodle can be used in this soup. Try to find interesting shapes that will appeal to your kids. Alphabet pasta is always a hit.

1 ½ tbsp canola oil

1 onion, diced

½ tsp dried thyme

2 stalks celery, diced

2 to 3 carrots, sliced

½ sweet red pepper, seeded and diced

2 dried bay leaves

7 to 8 cups Homemade Salt-Free Chicken Stock (page 102), or salt-free or low-sodium canned chicken broth

2 chicken breasts, cooked and diced (or approximately 1 lb

or 500 g cooked chicken)
3 oz (84 g) dried pasta
1/2 cup peas
1/3 cup chopped fresh parsley
Kosher salt and freshly ground pepper

- Heat oil in large stockpot over medium heat. Add onion and thyme and sauté for 5 minutes.
- Add celery, carrots, peppers and bay leaves and sauté for another 5 minutes. Add 7 cups of chicken stock and bring to boil. Reduce heat and simmer with lid partially on for 10 minutes. Stir occasionally.
- Add chicken and pasta and continue to simmer for another 10 minutes or until pasta is al dente. Add peas and parsley and continue to simmer for 5 minutes.
- Remove bay leaves and add salt and pepper to taste. If soup seems too thick, add extra stock as desired.

*Yield: 8 to 10 cups*

Soups

## Broccoli and Cheddar Cheese Soup

Because this soup is made with frozen broccoli, it is a snap to make. Take care not to boil the soup once the cheese has been added, or the soup will separate.

2 tbsp canola oil
1 onion, diced
1 tsp chopped fresh thyme
1 garlic clove, minced
2 pkgs (1 lb/500 g each) frozen broccoli
1/2 pkg (5 oz/150 g) frozen spinach
8 to 9 cups Homemade Salt-Free Chicken Stock (page 102), or salt-free or low-sodium chicken broth
2 cups packed, shredded aged Cheddar cheese, plus an

extra few tbsp for garnish
Kosher salt and freshly ground pepper

- Heat oil in large stockpot over medium-low heat. Add onions, thyme and garlic and sauté for 7 to 10 minutes, stirring frequently to ensure garlic doesn't burn and onions don't brown.
- Add broccoli, spinach and 8 cups chicken stock and bring to boil. Reduce heat and simmer for 15 minutes.
- With hand-held immersion blender, purée soup until smooth.
- Gradually add 2 cups Cheddar cheese and stir until melted. Simmer for another 5 minutes. Add salt and pepper to taste. If soup seems too thick, add extra chicken stock as desired.
- Serve soup topped with garnish of Cheddar cheese.

*Yield: Approximately 10 to 12 cups*

## Bone Up on Calcium

Calcium is an essential dietary nutrient needed for the building of healthy bones and teeth, as well as the proper functioning of the heart, muscles and nerves. The teenage years are a period of rapid bone growth, and therefore the need for calcium almost doubles during this period. However, we know that one third of children aged 4 to 9 do not get the recommended number of servings of dairy products per day, and these numbers have a tendency to get worse as children progress through adolescence.[28] Inadequate calcium intake during childhood cannot be made up for later in life. This is because 90 per cent of adult bone mass has been laid down by the time the average teen finishes his growth spurt (around 17 to 18 years of age). Insufficient calcium intake during childhood increases the risk of both fractures and developing osteoporosis later in life. In fact, many doctors believe the increase in childhood forearm fractures is a direct result of inadequate calcium intake.

Help your children develop strong bones by ensuring they get the calcium they need. Children should drink at least 2 cups of lower fat milk (skim, 1% or 2%) or fortified soy beverage every day and eat a wide variety of calcium-rich foods. These foods include dairy products, canned salmon (with bones), leafy greens, broccoli, baked beans and chickpeas, as well as calcium-fortified foods such as tofu and orange juice.

## Italian Meatball Soup

When the meatballs are already made, this soup is very quick to put together.

2 tbsp canola oil
1 small onion, diced
2 carrots, sliced
1 tsp ground cumin
4 to 5 cups Homemade Salt-Free Chicken Stock (page 102), or salt-free or low-sodium chicken broth
1 ½ cups chopped kale
12 Lamb Meatballs (page 85)
Kosher salt and freshly ground pepper

- Heat oil in large saucepan over medium heat. Add onions and sauté for 5 minutes.
- Add carrots and cumin and sauté for another 5 minutes. Add 4 cups chicken stock and kale and stir thoroughly. Bring to rapid boil. Reduce heat and add meatballs. Simmer with lid mostly on for 20 minutes.
- Add salt and pepper to taste. If soup seems too thick, add extra stock as desired.

*Yield: 8 cups*

# Carrot Spaghetti Squash Soup

Because the squash is cooked in the microwave, this soup is very easy to make. The flavour is fairly mild and should appeal to young children. If you prefer a spicier version, you could add 1 tsp of crushed red-pepper flakes, or a little hot sauce to the adults' portions.

¼ cup canola oil
4 large carrots, grated
1 large onion, diced
4 garlic cloves, minced
1 tsp dried thyme
1 large spaghetti squash (over 3 lbs or 1 ½ kg)
6 to 8 cups Homemade Salt-Free Chicken Stock (page 102),
   or salt-free or low-sodium chicken broth
½ cup chopped fresh parsley (optional)
Kosher salt and freshly ground pepper

- Heat oil in large stockpot over medium heat. Add carrots, onions, garlic and thyme and sauté for approximately 5 to 10 minutes, or until softened, being careful not to burn garlic.
- Using tip of knife, pierce squash in 4 places. Place in microwave and cook on high for 10 minutes.
- Cut squash in half lengthways. Using large spoon, gently scrape out seeds and discard. Using fork, scrape spaghetti-like strands of squash into bowl.
- Add squash to carrot mixture and continue to sauté for another 15 minutes.
- With hand-held immersion blender, purée vegetables until smooth. Add 6 cups chicken stock, stirring thoroughly, and bring to boil. Reduce heat and simmer for 20 minutes.
- Remove from heat and add parsley (if using) and salt and pepper to taste. If soup seems too thick, add more stock as desired.

*Yield: Approximately 10 cups*

## Roasted Tomato and Red Pepper Soup

This is our favourite soup from *The Good Food Book for Families*, so we just had to include it. If you cannot find Roma tomatoes, substitute regular ones.

3 lbs (1 ½ kg) Roma tomatoes, quartered and seeded
3 lbs (1 ½ kg) sweet red bell peppers, halved and seeded
¼ cup canola oil, 2 tbsp canola oil, plus an extra drizzle
1 head garlic, topped
1 onion, diced
4 carrots, grated
7 to 8 cups Homemade Salt-Free Chicken Stock (page 102),
    or salt-free or low-sodium chicken broth
Kosher salt and freshly ground pepper

- Preheat oven to 350°F. Line 2 baking sheets with foil or parchment paper.
- Lay tomatoes and red peppers on baking sheets and drizzle with ¼ cup oil. Drizzle a little more oil over garlic, wrap in foil and place on baking sheet. Bake tomatoes, peppers and garlic for 45 minutes.
- Heat remaining 2 tbsp oil in large stockpot over medium heat. Add onions and carrots and sauté for 10 minutes, or until soft.
- Remove vegetables from oven. Unwrap garlic and let cool. Squeeze garlic onto tomatoes and discard skin. The edges of peppers will likely have blackened. If so, cut these edges off and discard blackened bits.
- Add roasted vegetables to stockpot and sauté for 5 minutes. Using hand-held immersion blender, purée vegetables until smooth. (If you do not have handheld immersion blender, remove vegetables from pot and purée in food processor or blender until smooth.)
- Add 7 cups chicken stock, stirring thoroughly, and bring to boil. Reduce heat and simmer for 20 minutes.

Soups

- Add salt and pepper to taste. If soup seems too thick, add extra stock as desired.

*Yield: Approximately 10 cups*

## Japanese Udon Noodle Soup

Once the vegetables are prepped, this soup takes less than 10 minutes to make, which means you can cut up the vegetables the night before and cook this soup in the morning while the children eat their breakfast. Or you can make it entirely the night before and refrigerate it overnight.

> 4 cups Homemade Salt-Free Chicken Stock (page 102), or salt-free or low-sodium chicken broth
> 2 1/3 tbsp low-sodium soy sauce
> 1 1/2 tsp freshly grated ginger
> 1 tsp brown sugar
> 1 star anise (optional)
> 1 package 7 oz / 200 g udon noodles
> 1 cup chopped bok choy
> 1 carrot, grated
> 1/2 cup button mushrooms, thinly sliced
> 1/2 cup sugar snap peas, ends and stringy bits removed, and chopped into 1/4-inch pieces
> 4 oz / 112 g firm tofu, diced
> 2 tbsp chopped fresh cilantro

- In large saucepan over medium-high heat, combine chicken stock, soy sauce, ginger, brown sugar and star anise (if using). Bring to boil and add noodles. Reduce heat to low and simmer for 3 minutes.
- Add bok choy, carrot, mushrooms, sugar snap peas and tofu and stir. Simmer for 2 to 3 minutes, or until vegetables are tender-crisp.
- Remove from heat and add cilantro.

*Yield: Serves 3 to 4*

# 6.

## Super Salads

High in dietary fibre and packed full of vegetables, salads are a healthy addition to any lunch box. Because the typical salad contains 2, 3 or even 4 servings of Vegetables and Fruit, packing a salad is a wonderful way to boost your child's intake of this important food group.

The key to a good lunch box salad is keeping it fresh and crisp. Use an ice pack to keep the salad cool and choose vegetables that retain their crunch, such as carrots, sweet peppers, cucumbers, celery, shredded cabbage, romaine lettuce and radishes. When adding greens, be sure to pack the dressing on the side to prevent the lettuce from wilting.

This chapter is divided into 2 sections: One Pot Salads and Dinner Salads. Our One Pot Salads are specifically designed for lunch boxes and come in single serving portions, whereas our Dinner Salads are made in larger portions and can last in the refrigerator for several days.

To help with the morning rush, our salad recipes outline what can be done the night before.

## One Pot Salads

Whether served with a whole grain roll and a slice of cheese, half a sandwich or a Thermos of soup, our One Pot Salads are sure to be a hit.

### Kid's One Pot Green Salad

Any vegetable can be added to this salad—what we've included are merely suggestions. Chop up a variety of veggies and get your kids to make their own salads. Remember, children are more likely to eat food that they have helped prepare. To add a boost of protein, sprinkle a few chickpeas, a few black beans, a few cubes of chicken or even some shredded Cheddar cheese on the salad.

1 ½ cups chopped mixed dark green salad greens (such as arugula, romaine, green leaf lettuce or spinach)
½ cup assorted vegetables, such as:
    Radishes, thinly sliced or diced
    Carrot, grated
    Canned corn, drained and rinsed
    Celery, diced
    Cabbage, shredded

Sweet red or green pepper, seeded and diced
Cherry tomatoes, halved
Cucumber, seeded and diced
Green onion, thinly sliced
1 ½ tbsp Orange Honey Dressing (below) or your child's
favourite alternative

• The night before, place mixed dark green lettuces in reusable container. Add assorted vegetables on top. Pour dressing into separate leak-proof container and refrigerate it and salad overnight.

*Yield: Serves 1*

## Orange Honey Dressing

This is Brenda's kids' favourite salad dressing. Extra dressing can be stored in the refrigerator for a week.

2 tbsp orange juice concentrate
2 tbsp apple cider vinegar
2 tbsp canola oil
1 tbsp honey
2 tsp Dijon mustard
Kosher salt and freshly ground pepper

• In small bowl, whisk together first 5 ingredients until combined. Add salt and pepper to taste.

*Yield: Approximately ½ cup*

Super Salads

## One Pot BC Salade Niçoise

Although this salad can be made with canned salmon, it's best made with fresh, so plan for extra salmon when cooking dinner. Try Barbecued Asian Salmon (page 155), which is a favourite at Cheryl's house.

2 cups chopped mixed dark green salad greens (such as romaine, arugula and spinach)

8 green beans, steamed for approximately 3 minutes until tender-crisp, rinsed under cold water, dried and chopped into 1-inch segments

3 baby potatoes, boiled just until tender, quartered

1 tbsp finely diced red onion (optional)

2 ½ tbsp White Balsamic Vinaigrette (below)

2 oz / 56 g cooked salmon (leftover from dinner or canned)

4 cherry tomatoes, halved

• The night before, place mixed salad greens in reusable container. Top with green beans, potatoes and onions (if using). Pour dressing into separate leak-proof container and refrigerate it and salad overnight.

• In the morning, place salmon and tomatoes on top of salad.

*Yield: Serves 1*

## White Balsamic Vinaigrette

This dressing is Brenda's favourite. The extra dressing can be stored in the refrigerator for a week.

¼ cup white balsamic vinegar

1 tbsp Dijon mustard

1 garlic clove, minced

½ cup extra-virgin olive oil

Kosher salt and freshly ground pepper

- In small bowl, whisk together vinegar, Dijon mustard and garlic. Slowly whisk in oil until combined. Add salt and pepper to taste.

*Yield: Approximately ¾ cup*

## Go Wild for Wild Salmon

While both wild and farmed salmon are good sources of heart healthy omega-3 fatty acids, we recommend choosing wild salmon whenever possible. The wild variety of salmon is both healthier and easier on the environment than farmed. Wild salmon contains lower levels of chemical contaminants, including PCBs, which have been linked to increased rates of cancer and birth defects.[29] Farmed salmon are given drugs, pesticides and antibiotics. In fact, farmed salmon receive more antibiotics by weight than any other livestock,[30] and this may, in part, be contributing to the rise of antibiotic-resistant disease.

Most farmed salmon is raised in densely packed floating cages, and the impact of these farms on the natural ecosystem is devastating. Salmon farms pollute coastal waters with drug-laden waste from feces and excess food. Disease and parasites pass through the cages infecting and depleting wild stocks. Escaped salmon further the spread of disease and may displace wild stocks in their natural habitat. Because salmon are carnivores, the farmers are depleting natural fish stocks in order to create salmon feed. In fact, it takes 2 to 4 kg of wild feed to produce 1 kg of salmon.[31]

When purchasing salmon, always confirm that it is wild. If salmon is labelled "Atlantic" it is farmed. Sockeye, chum and pink are not farmed. Coho and chinook are available in farmed and wild varieties. Canned salmon, an economical choice, is usually wild, but check the label. In most cases, sending a canned salmon sandwich to school is a healthy and environmentally friendly choice.

Super Salads

## One Pot Kid's Cobb Salad

A traditional Cobb salad is made with blue cheese instead of Cheddar, so use that if your child likes it.

1 ½ cups chopped romaine lettuce
2 tbsp shredded Cheddar cheese
1 tomato, seeded and diced
1/4 cup diced cooked chicken breast
1 slice bacon, cooked crisp and crumbled (optional)
1 ½ tbsp White Balsamic Vinaigrette (page 128) or your
  child's favourite dressing
¼ avocado, diced
1 squeeze fresh lemon juice

- The night before, toss lettuce and cheese together and place in reusable container. Prep tomato, chicken and bacon (if using). Pour dressing into separate leak-proof container. Refrigerate overnight.
- In the morning, place chicken in strip in centre of salad. Place tomatoes in strip next to chicken.
- In small bowl, toss avocado with lemon juice, and place in strip next to chicken. Scatter bacon over salad.

*Yield: Serves 1*

## One Pot Greek Salad

Most kids love Greek salad. Served with Toasted Whole Wheat Pita Chips (page 88), a little Minted Tzatziki (page 97) and Homemade Hummus (page 97), it makes a healthy lunch.

1 ½ tbsp extra-virgin olive oil
½ rounded tsp dried oregano
½ English cucumber, seeded and cut into ¾-inch chunks
½ sweet green pepper, seeded and cut into ¾-inch chunks

Super Salads

5 kalamata olives
1 ¼ oz/35 g chunk feta cheese, crumbled
1 tbsp finely diced red onion (optional)
Kosher salt and freshly ground pepper
6 cherry or grape tomatoes, halved

- The night before, place olive oil and oregano in small bowl. Add cucumbers, green peppers, olives, cheese and onions (if using) and toss to coat. Add salt and pepper to taste and pack in reusable container. Refrigerate overnight.
- In the morning, add tomatoes and toss.

*Yield: Serves 1*

## What about Pesticides on Produce?

The decision whether or not to choose organic produce is a personal one and there are many factors that need to be considered. Given that 70 per cent of children are not eating the recommended number of servings of fruit and vegetables per day,[32] the vast majority of Canadians would improve their diet and their health by eating more produce, organic or not.

Be assured that, to date, there is little evidence to suggest organic produce is safer or more nutritious in any meaningful way. However, some fruit and vegetables do carry higher pesticide loads. As a general rule, fruit and vegetables with thicker skins (for example onions and watermelon) have lower pesticide loads. For an up-to-date list of produce with high and low pesticide loads, turn to Appendix II (page 195). It may make sense to use this list as a guide when shopping. Regardless of what you decide, you can minimize your exposure to pesticides by thoroughly washing all produce under cold running water and avoiding fruit and vegetables with cuts or insect holes.

Another factor to consider in your decision is that organic farming is generally believed to be better for the environment than conventional farms—organic farms use less energy, produce less waste and do not release synthetic chemicals into the environment. Synthetic pesticides and fertilizers are often made with fossil fuels and transporting and manufacturing these chemicals uses energy and produces greenhouse gases. Not surprisingly, studies have shown that chemical farming uses significantly more energy per unit of production than organic farms.[33] However, there are times when organic produce isn't always better. When faced with buying organic strawberries from California or seasonal, local berries, choose local. Not only is local food fresher, it tastes better and is easier on the environment. As the distance between the food and fork increases, so does the use of fossil fuels needed to transport the food.

## One Pot Turkey Taco Salad

This is a delicious way to use up leftover Black Bean Turkey Tacos (page 151) from last night's dinner.

1 1/2 cups chopped romaine lettuce
1 tomato, seeded and diced
3 tbsp shredded Cheddar cheese
1/3 rounded cup Black Bean Turkey Taco mixture (page 151)
3 tbsp salsa

- In reusable container, combine lettuce, tomatoes and cheese. In separate leak-proof container, combine Black Bean Turkey Taco mixture and salsa and mix to combine. Refrigerate overnight.
- At school, your child pours turkey mixture over salad and enjoys!

*Yield: Serves 1*

## One Pot Melon Ball Salad

For best results this salad should be made in the morning. If you don't have a melon baller, just cut the fruit into 1-inch cubes.

5 balls watermelon
5 balls cantaloupe
5 balls honeydew melon
I squeeze fresh lime juice or to taste
½ tsp fresh mint, finely chopped
Approximately ¼ tsp granulated sugar

- In reusable leak-proof container, combine watermelon, cantaloupe, honeydew, lime juice, mint and sugar. Taste and add more lime juice or sugar as desired.

*Yield: Serves 1*

Super Salads

## Dinner Salads

Dinner salads or, dare we say, leftover salads, are larger than one pot salads. They can be served for dinner, will last in the refrigerator for several days and tend to travel well. Dinner salads have the added advantage of being packed full of beans, whole grains and pasta, complex carbohydrates that supply a steady stream of slow-release energy. Since complex carbohydrates take longer to break down, they'll keep your child feeling full a little longer.

To save precious morning minutes, all of the salads in this section can be made the night before and stored in the refrigerator until morning.

## Kid's Pesto Pasta Salad

1 head broccoli, cut into bite-sized florets
(approximately 3 cups)
4 cups fusilli pasta
6 tbsp Homemade Pesto (page 61), or store-bought
equivalent
25 cherry tomatoes, halved and sprinkled with kosher salt
1 cup frozen peas, cooked
1 cup baby carrots, sliced
2 tbsp finely chopped fresh basil

- Bring large pot of water to boil. Add broccoli and cook 2 to 3 minutes, or until broccoli is tender-crisp. Drain and rinse under cold water. Drain again and set aside.
- Bring large pot of salted water to boil. Add pasta and cook until al dente. Drain and rinse under cold water. Drain again.
- In large bowl, toss pasta with pesto, reserved broccoli, tomatoes, peas, carrots and fresh basil.

*Yield: Serves 6*

## Mediterranean Bulgur Salad

1 cup bulgur
1 cup boiling water
20 cherry tomatoes, halved
1 English cucumber, seeded and diced
1 rounded cup canned chickpeas, drained and rinsed, or
cooked chickpeas
1/3 cup finely diced red onion
1 bunch chopped fresh parsley (approximately 1 cup)
1/3 cup chopped fresh mint

3 tbsp olive oil
2 tbsp fresh lemon juice
2 garlic cloves, minced
Kosher salt and freshly ground pepper

- Place bulgur in bowl, pour boiling water over it, and stir with fork. Place foil directly on surface of bulgur and let sit for 30 minutes.
- Fluff bulgur with fork and drain if necessary to remove excess liquid.
- In large salad bowl, combine bulgur, tomatoes, cucumber, chickpeas, onions, parsley and mint.
- In small bowl, whisk together olive oil, lemon juice, garlic, and salt and pepper to taste. Pour over bulgur and mix thoroughly. Serve salad at room temperature or store in refrigerator for up to 2 days.

*Yield: Serves 6 to 8*

Super Salads

### Go Loco for Local Produce

Make a concerted effort to minimize your environmental footprint by serving seasonal, local produce whenever possible. Encourage your children to read labels and find out where their food comes from. How much sense does it make to buy apples from New Zealand when we grow fabulous ones in Canada? Why eat a banana in the summer when a delicious selection of local fruits and berries are in season? Support your local farmers' market. To find out where it is, go to www.farmers marketscanada.ca. You can also ask your grocer to bring in local produce. Doing so not only reduces the environmental cost of food, it also helps to support Canadian farmers, which in turn helps to preserve precious farmland around our cities.

One of the best ways to obtain local produce is to grow it yourself. Vegetable gardens are the perfect way to teach your children about the connection between nature and food, while reducing both your food bill and carbon footprint. Moreover, there is no better way to entice children to eat their vegetables than getting them involved in a vegetable garden.

Not only is seasonal local produce easier on the environment, it tastes better and is generally more nutritious. Once picked, the vitamins and minerals in fruits and vegetables begin to deteriorate. Generally, the longer produce has to travel, the more time it has to deteriorate.

## Chickpea Tabbouleh

To boost the veggie content and colour of this salad, you can add a seeded and diced sweet red pepper.

I can (19 oz/540 mL) chickpeas, drained and rinsed,
  or 2 cups cooked chickpeas
I bunch chopped fresh flat leaf parsley
  (approximately I cup)
$1/3$ cup chopped fresh mint
$1/2$ English cucumber, seeded and diced
2 tbsp red onion, finely diced
$1/2$ cup crumbled feta cheese
$1/2$ cup Lemon Shallot Dressing (below)

• In bowl, combine ingredients thoroughly. Serve immediately or store in refrigerator for several days.

*Yield: Approximately 4 servings*

## Lemon Shallot Dressing

According to Chef James Schaeffer, the creator of this dressing, the key is to use a sharp knife to dice the shallots. A dull knife runs the risk of bruising the shallots, which can muddy the dressing.

I tbsp finely diced shallots
2 tbsp fresh lemon juice

½ cup canola oil
Kosher salt and white pepper

- In small bowl, combine shallots and lemon juice. Slowly whisk in oil until combined. Add salt and pepper to taste.

*Yield: Almost ¾ cup*

## Chickpeas

Like most beans, chickpeas (also called garbanzo beans), are a good source of protein, cholesterol-lowering fibre and folate, the nutrient proven to prevent spinal cord defects in newborns. Chickpeas are also an excellent source of magnesium. Magnesium is one of the most abundant minerals in the body and is needed for over 300 biochemical reactions. It is needed to build strong bones, maintain normal muscle and nerve function, support a healthy immune system, help regulate blood pressure and keep our heart rhythm steady. However, we know that approximately 50 per cent of teens have an inadequate intake of magnesium.[34] To ensure your teen doesn't become part of this statistic, serve a wide variety of magnesium-rich foods such as halibut, almonds, soybeans, oatmeal and green vegetables.

## Italian-Style Orzo Salad

At any summer barbecue, this salad looks great on the picnic table. Be careful not to overcook the orzo—mushy pasta is the fastest way to ruin a good pasta salad. This recipe makes a fairly large quantity, and any extra can be stored in the refrigerator for several days.

To turn this salad into an entree, add a couple of cans of tuna.

½ cup extra-virgin olive oil
2 tbsp fresh lemon juice
1 tsp lemon zest
2 cups orzo pasta

10 shallots, sliced (approximately 3 cups)
1/3 cup balsamic vinegar
2 cans (14 oz/398 mL each) artichoke hearts packed in
  water, drained, rinsed and quartered
3 garlic cloves, minced
3/4 cup pitted and chopped kalamata olives
15 sun-dried tomatoes packed in oil, diced
1 sweet red pepper, seeded and diced
1 cup chopped fresh cilantro
1 cup chopped fresh parsley
1/3 cup chopped fresh mint
1 cup crumbled feta cheese
Kosher salt and freshly ground pepper

- In large bowl, combine 4 tbsp oil, lemon juice and zest.
- Bring large pot of salted water to boil. Add orzo and cook until al dente. Drain and rinse under cold water. Drain again.
- Toss orzo with oil and lemon juice mixture and set aside.
- Heat remaining 4 tbsp oil in skillet over medium heat. Add shallots and sauté for 5 minutes. Add balsamic vinegar and sauté for 5 minutes. Add artichokes and garlic and sauté for another 5 minutes. Add shallot and artichoke mixture to orzo.
- Add olives, sun-dried tomatoes, red pepper, cilantro, parsley, mint and feta cheese to reserved orzo and mix thoroughly. If salad seems a little dry, add extra drizzle of olive oil and toss to coat. Add salt and pepper to taste.

*Yield: Serves 10 to 12*

**Sprout Warning**

Bean sprouts should not be a part of your child's lunch box. Bean sprouts provide the perfect breeding ground for bacteria and, as a result, have been linked to a number of outbreaks of both salmonella and E. coli. Because of this, Health Canada advises young children, senior citizens and people with weak immune systems to avoid raw sprouts altogether.[35]

## Mediterranean Bean Salad

Admittedly this salad is rather sophisticated for the average child's lunch box, but we love it so much we decided to include it anyway.

Super Salads

1 can (19 oz/540 mL) chickpeas, drained and rinsed, or 2 cups cooked chickpeas

1 can (19 oz/540 mL) black beans, drained and rinsed, or 2 cups cooked black beans

1 can (14 oz/398 mL) artichoke hearts packed in water, drained, rinsed and diced

1 sweet red pepper, seeded and diced

2 cups chopped kale

15 kalamata olives, pitted and chopped

8 sun-dried tomatoes, diced

3/4 cup crumbled feta cheese

1/2 cup Balsamic Vinaigrette (page 140)

In large bowl, combine all ingredients.

*Yield: Serves 6 to 8*

# Balsamic Vinaigrette

¼ cup balsamic vinegar
2 tsp Dijon mustard
1 garlic clove, minced
½ cup extra-virgin olive oil
Kosher salt and freshly ground pepper

• In small bowl, combine balsamic vinegar, mustard and garlic. Slowly whisk in oil until combined. Add salt and pepper to taste.

*Yield: ¾ cup*

## Winter Greens

In an effort to eat seasonal local produce, many Canadians are turning to winter greens such as kale, Swiss chard, mustard greens, turnip greens and beet greens. Not only are these vegetables low in calories and virtually fat free, they are packed full of nutrients, including vitamins A, C and K as well as folate, calcium, iron, potassium and fibre. What's more, these vegetables are an exceptional source of disease-fighting phytochemicals such as beta carotene and lutein. An easy way to include winter greens in your child's lunch box is to chop them up and add them to homemade soups, or try Mediterranean Bean Salad (page 139).

# Karen's Greek Quinoa Salad

This is a delicious accompaniment to any lunch.

1½ cups quinoa, rinsed and drained
25 cherry tomatoes, halved
1 sweet green pepper, seeded and diced
¾ of an English cucumber, seeded and diced
⅓ cup kalamata olives, halved and pitted

¼ cup finely diced red onion
⅓ cup chopped fresh parsley
2 to 3 tbsp chopped fresh basil
2/3 cup crumbled goat's milk feta cheese
¼ cup Balsamic Vinaigrette (page 140)

- Bring large pot of water to boil. Add quinoa and cook for approximately 8 to 10 minutes, or until tender yet still slightly crunchy. Drain and spread on baking sheet to dry (approximately 5 minutes). Transfer to large bowl.
- Add tomatoes, green peppers, cucumber, olives, onions, parsley, 2 tbsp basil, feta cheese and dressing and toss to combine. Taste and add more basil if desired.

*Yield: Serves 6 to 8*

## The Magic of Quinoa

Quinoa, the ancient grain of the Incas, is sometimes called a super grain because of its high nutrient profile. Rich in protein, quinoa is an excellent source of essential amino acids, most notably lysine. Lysine, not found in other grains, is needed for the growth and repair of body tissue. Quinoa is also low in fat while being a good source of fibre, B vitamins and minerals, including magnesium, potassium and zinc. Immune function, cognitive function and behaviour are all dependent on adequate levels of zinc.

Quinoa is inexpensive, quick to cook and versatile. It is delicious hot or cold and can be substituted for rice in recipes.

# Mexican Quinoa Salad

1 cup quinoa, rinsed and drained

1 cup canned corn, drained and rinsed

1 cup canned black beans, drained and rinsed, or
  1 cup cooked black beans

25 cherry tomatoes, halved

1 bunch green onions, sliced

1 sweet red pepper, seeded and diced

1 cup chopped fresh cilantro

5 tbsp fresh lime juice

4 tbsp canola oil

2 large garlic cloves, minced

1 tsp ground cumin

Pinch of granulated sugar

2 large handfuls arugula, chopped

2 tbsp olive oil

Kosher salt and freshly ground pepper

- Bring large pot of water to boil. Add quinoa and cook for approximately 8 to 10 minutes, or until tender yet slightly crunchy. Drain and spread on baking sheet to dry (approximately 5 minutes). Transfer to large bowl.
- Add corn, black beans, tomatoes, green onions, red pepper and cilantro.
- In small bowl, combine lime juice, canola oil, garlic, cumin and sugar. Pour over quinoa mixture and toss to coat.
- Add arugula, olive oil and salt and pepper to taste, and toss again. Serve at room temperature or store in refrigerator for several days.

*Yield: Serves 6 to 8*

## Fish Boosts Brain Power

A recent large-scale study indicated that teenage boys who ate fish more than once a week tended to score higher on intelligence tests 3 years later.[36] Researchers believe this is of critical importance because the late-teen years are a key time for brain plasticity. Plasticity refers to the brain's ability to reorganize itself in response to novel experiences such as learning a skill or reacting to one's environment. The researchers believe it is the omega-3 fatty acids present in fish that act in several ways to improve brain function. Omega-3 fatty acids are especially highly concentrated in oily fish such as mackerel, salmon, trout and, to a lesser extent, tuna.

## Salade Niçoise

This recipe comes from *The Good Food Book for Families*. It makes an easy, last-minute dinner and, as an added benefit, leftovers can be sent to school the following day.

3/4 lb/375 g green beans, trimmed
1 1/4 1lb/625 g baby potatoes, quartered
20 cherry tomatoes, halved
1/2 cup Kalamata olives, pitted
1/4 red onion, thinly sliced
2 cans (6 oz/170 g each) low-sodium, light tuna, drained
1/2 cup White Balsamic Vinaigrette
4 hard-boiled eggs, quartered

- Blanch beans in boiling water until bright green, approximately 3 minutes. Drain, and plunge into ice bath to stop cooking process.
- Cook potatoes in boiling water until just tender. Drain well and let cool.
- In large bowl, combine green beans, potatoes, tomatoes, olives, onion, tuna and dressing until coated. Arrange salad on serving platter and place hard-boiled eggs around edges.

*Yield: Serves 4 to 6*

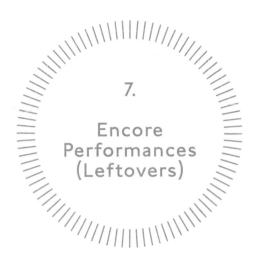

## 7.

## Encore Performances (Leftovers)

Planning for leftovers is a simple way to save time and add variety to your child's lunch box. Because most leftovers are prepped the night before, there is often little to do in the morning. Soups, stews, noodles, casseroles, chili and pasta are obvious easy choices. However, with a little forethought, most dinners can be packed for lunch. For example, to send your child's favourite roast beef or turkey dinner to school, just dice the meat and vegetables and store them with mashed or roasted potatoes in the refrigerator overnight. In the morning, heat them up. Pack the potatoes in a preheated Thermos, top with the vegetables and meat and drizzle with gravy. Leftover chicken and fish go well with steamed vegetables, whole grain rice and a drizzle of soy sauce. Investing in a timed rice maker is an easy way to ensure you always have fresh rice ready when you need it.

Packed in a Thermos, your child's favourite pasta makes an easy last-minute lunch. Just cook extra sauce with dinner, possibly doubling or tripling your recipe. Freeze the sauce in individual reusable containers or even ice cube trays: 3 to 4 cubes make approximately 1 portion of sauce. The night before, place the frozen cubes in the refrigerator to defrost. In the morning, heat the sauce in the microwave and cook pasta until al dente. The pasta should be a little undercooked because it will continue to cook in the Thermos. Toss the sauce with the pasta and pour it into a preheated Thermos. Young children tend to love pasta tossed with butter and a little grated Parmesan cheese too. Adding steamed peas or other leftover veggies boosts the nutritional content of this simple dish.

## Egg Fried Rice

This is another favourite of Brenda's son, Charlie. Although Egg Fried Rice can be made with either white rice or whole grain rice, use whole grain rice for the extra nutrients and fibre. Cold, leftover rice works best in this recipe as the grains are less inclined to stick together. However, in a pinch, warm rice can be used.

When you have leftover rice, this dish can be made while the children eat their breakfast, in less than 10 minutes! Alternatively you can make it for dinner, store the leftovers in the refrigerator and reheat them in the morning before packing them in a preheated Thermos.

Egg Fried Rice is the perfect way to use up leftover vegetables. Just substitute 1 cup of diced vegetables for the peas. If you want only a single portion of Egg Fried Rice, use these quantities: 1 tbsp soy sauce, 1 tbsp oyster sauce, 1½ tbsp canola oil, 1 egg, 1 cup rice, 1 small grated carrot, ½ cup frozen peas (or diced leftover veggies) and ½ of a green onion. If you would like to add some additional protein, add a little chicken or diced firm tofu.

2 tbsp oyster sauce

2 tbsp soy sauce

¼ cup canola oil

3 eggs, beaten

3 cups cooked rice

1 cup frozen peas (or diced leftover veggies)

½ cup grated carrot

2 green onions, thinly sliced (optional)

- In small bowl, whisk together oyster sauce and soy sauce to combine. Set aside.
- Heat 1 tsp oil in large skillet. Add eggs and scramble them as they cook for 1 to 2 minutes.
- Add rice and remaining oil and stir-fry for 3 minutes.
- Add peas, carrots and green onions and sauté for 2 to 3 minutes, or until well combined and warmed through.

*Yield: Serves 4*

## Minted Lamb Ragout

Kids love spaghetti and bolognese sauce, and this variation, made with lamb, is a nice alternative. If you want to make a more traditional ragout, simply substitute beef for the lamb and fresh basil for the mint, and add 1 tbsp of dried oregano to the pot when sautéing the vegetables.

This recipe makes a fairly large quantity of sauce to conveniently provide leftovers that can be frozen in individual containers for lunch. Defrost the sauce in the refrigerator overnight. In the morning, heat the sauce and cook some pasta until al dente.

Toss the cooked pasta with the sauce and pour it into a preheated Thermos.

| | |
|---|---|
| ⅓ cup canola oil | 1 ½ cans (28 oz/796 mL |
| 2 lbs (1 kg) ground lamb | each) diced tomatoes |
| ½ tsp each kosher salt and | 2 dried bay leaves |
| freshly ground pepper | ¾ cup fresh mint, chopped |
| 3 carrots | ½ cup ricotta cheese |
| 2 stalks celery | Kosher salt and freshly |
| 1 large onion | ground pepper to taste |
| 1 shallot | Cooked spaghetti (enough |
| 3 garlic cloves | for your family's dinner) |
| 1 cup red wine | ⅓ cup grated Parmesan |
| 1 can (5 ½ oz/156 mL) | cheese, approximately |
| tomato paste | |

- In large stockpot, heat 1 tbsp oil over medium heat. Add lamb, salt and pepper and cook for 10 minutes, or until no longer pink. Drain off fat and remove lamb to plate.
- In bowl of food processor, place carrots, celery, onions, shallots and garlic and process until finely chopped.
- In stockpot, heat remaining ¼ cup oil. Add onion mixture and sauté for 10 minutes.
- Return lamb to stockpot, add wine and continue to sauté for another 10 minutes.
- Add tomato paste and stir to combine. Add tomatoes and bay leaves, and bring to boil. Reduce heat and simmer for approximately 20 minutes, or until flavours are blended.
- Add mint and ricotta and stir to combine. Add salt and pepper to taste. To serve, remove bay leaves and spoon ragout over cooked pasta. Top with freshly grated Parmesan cheese.

*Yield: 10 cups*

## Penne with Two-Cheese Tomato Sauce

This sauce is also delicious tossed with steamed asparagus and pitted kalamata olives. If you prefer a plain tomato sauce, simply omit the cheese in this recipe. Extra sauce can be frozen in individual containers for lunch. To defrost, place in the refrigerator overnight. In the morning, heat the sauce and cook pasta until al dente. Toss the sauce and pasta together and pour into a preheated Thermos.

2 tbsp olive oil
I large onion, diced
4 garlic cloves, minced
1½ cans (28 oz/796 mL each) diced tomatoes
I can (5½ oz/156 mL) tomato paste
½ cup water
¾ cup chopped fresh basil

¼ cup goat's cheese, firmly packed
½ cup grated Parmesan cheese, plus extra for serving at table
Kosher salt and freshly ground pepper
Cooked penne pasta (enough for your family's dinner)

- Heat oil in large saucepan over medium heat. Add onions and garlic and sauté for approximately 8 minutes, or until onions are softened. Be careful not to burn the garlic.
- Add diced tomatoes, tomato paste and water and stir to combine. Bring to boil.
- Reduce heat, add ½ cup basil and simmer for 30 minutes, stirring occasionally.
- Slowly crumble in goat's cheese and add Parmesan cheese. Stir until melted. Add salt and pepper to taste.
- To serve, toss sauce with cooked pasta and remaining ¼ cup basil. Serve with extra Parmesan cheese.

*Yield: 8 cups*

# Brenda's Chicken Curry

This recipe calls for 1 to 1½ tsp of cayenne pepper, which produces a fairly spicy curry. If you prefer a milder version, start with 1 tsp and add a little more if desired. Alternatively, make the curry with 1 tsp of cayenne pepper and sprinkle a few crushed red-pepper flakes or some hot sauce on the adults' portions just prior to serving. If you cannot find garam masala, use 1 tsp of medium curry powder instead.

To pack this for lunch, place leftover curry and rice together in a reusable container and refrigerate overnight. In the morning, reheat it in the microwave and spoon it into a preheated Thermos.

1 cup plain Greek-style yogurt (or any plain yogurt above 3% milk fat)

2 tbsp fresh lemon juice

10 garlic cloves, minced

1 tbsp freshly grated ginger

2 tsp ground coriander

2 tsp ground cumin

1½ tsp garam masala

1 to 1½ tsp cayenne pepper

½ tsp ground turmeric

1 tsp kosher salt

3 lbs (1½ kg) chicken (skinless, boneless breasts and thighs), cut into cubes

3 tbsp canola oil

1 large onion, diced

1 jalapeño pepper, seeded and diced

⅓ cup tomato paste

2 tsp cumin seeds

2 to 3 cups Homemade Salt-Free Chicken Stock (page 102), or salt-free or low-sodium canned chicken broth

4 large carrots, sliced thickly

3 medium potatoes, peeled and cut into chunks

3 tbsp light cream cheese

1 cup frozen peas

½ cup fresh chopped cilantro

Cooked whole grain rice (enough for dinner plus extra for lunch the next day)

Encore Performances

- In large bowl, combine yogurt, lemon juice, garlic, ginger, coriander, cumin, garam masala, cayenne, turmeric and salt. Add chicken and toss to coat in yogurt mixture. Cover and refrigerate for at least 2 hours or as long as overnight.
- Heat 1 tbsp oil in large stockpot over medium heat. Add onions and jalapeño peppers and sauté for 5 minutes. Add remaining 2 tbsp of oil and chicken and sauté for approximately 10 minutes, or until chicken is browned.
- Add tomato paste and cumin seeds and stir to combine. Add 2 cups of chicken stock and mix thoroughly. Add carrots and potatoes and bring to boil.
- Reduce heat, add cream cheese and stir until melted. Simmer for approximately 25 minutes, or until vegetables are tender.
- Add peas and continue to simmer for another 5 minutes.
- Remove from heat, add cilantro and stir. The consistency should be that of a thick stew. Add more stock if needed. Serve over whole grain rice and enjoy!

*Yield: Serves 6*

## Black Bean Turkey Tacos

Leftovers from this dinner can be used to make a Black Bean Turkey Taco Wrap (page 71) or a One Pot Turkey Taco Salad (page 132) for lunch the next day.

2 tbsp canola oil
1 cup diced onion
2 stalks celery, diced
1 carrot, grated
2 garlic cloves, minced
1 lb (500 g) ground turkey
1 cup canned black beans, drained and rinsed, or cooked
    black beans

1 can (5½ oz/156 mL) tomato paste
2 tbsp chili powder
1 tsp ground cumin
2 cups water
½ cup chopped cilantro (optional)
Kosher salt and freshly ground pepper
14 10-inch whole wheat soft flour tortillas

Toppings:
1 cup salsa
1 cup light sour cream or plain Greek-style yogurt
10 leaves romaine lettuce, shredded
4 tomatoes, diced
⅓ cup diced red onion
1 avocado, diced
1 rounded cup shredded Cheddar cheese

- Heat oil in large skillet over medium heat. Add onions, celery, carrots and garlic and sauté for approximately 10 minutes, or until vegetables are softened.
- Crumble in ground turkey and sauté for 10 minutes, or until turkey is browned.
- Add black beans, tomato paste, chili powder, cumin and water. Simmer for 15 minutes, or until much of water has evaporated and flavours have combined.
- Remove from heat and add cilantro (if using) and salt and pepper to taste.
- To serve, spoon 2 tbsp of turkey mixture onto each tortilla and let everyone to choose their own toppings. Fold tacos over and enjoy!

*Yield: Serves 7 (2 tacos per person)*

## Overfed but Undernourished

Today children are consuming more high-calorie, low-nutrient foods than ever before. These foods include chips, candy, soda pop and fast food, as well as packaged cookies, cakes and baked goods. They tend to be full of refined carbohydrates (white flour and sugar), which break down quickly when eaten, resulting in a sudden spike in blood sugar and a quick burst of energy. But soon there is a crash, which leaves children feeling depleted and hungry.

Excess consumption of processed foods can lead to overeating and have a negative impact on both concentration and learning. So pack your child's lunch box full of complex carbohydrates like fruit, vegetables, whole grains and legumes. These foods supply a steady stream of energy that gets children through the day.

## Falafel

Admittedly falafels are a bit fussy to make, but they are certainly worth the extra effort and this recipe makes a fairly large quantity. Extra falafels can be stored in the refrigerator or freezer, providing convenient lunches for several days. If sending falafels to school, be sure to seed and dice the tomatoes and use the lettuce as a barrier to prevent the tzatziki from seeping into the pita bread. Alternatively, you can make falafel wraps, which are less likely to get soggy.

Be sure to use canola oil in this recipe as it has a high smoke point, which means that it won't burn as quickly as other oils do.

I medium onion, cut into chunks
4 garlic cloves, minced
2½ cans (19 oz/540 mL each) chickpeas, drained and rinsed,
   or 5 cups cooked chickpeas
I egg, beaten
I bunch fresh cilantro, chopped
I½ tsp ground cumin
I tsp kosher salt

½ tsp freshly ground pepper

¼ cup (approximately) canola oil

1 package whole wheat pita pockets (or enough for your
family and a few more for tomorrow's lunch)

½ head romaine lettuce, leaves separated

1 ½ cups Minted Tzatziki (page 97)


Toppings:

4 tomatoes, seeded and diced

½ cucumber, seeded and diced

¼ onion, diced

1 pickle, cut into thin strips

½ cup Homemade Hummus (page 97) or store-bought
equivalent

- In bowl of food processor, place onion and garlic and pulse until finely chopped. Transfer to large bowl.
- Reserve 1 cup whole chickpeas and place in same bowl. Place rest of chickpeas in bowl of food processor and purée until slightly grainy in consistency. (Depending on size of food processor, you may have to do this in batches.) Transfer puréed chickpeas to same bowl, and add egg, cilantro, cumin, salt and pepper. Mix until combined.
- Roll 2 tbsp of chickpea mixture into ball. Repeat with rest of chickpea mixture.
- Heat 1 tbsp oil in large, non-stick skillet over medium heat until drops of water sizzle in oil. Be careful not to burn oil. If it smokes, it is burning and needs to be replaced.
- Working in batches, place falafel balls in skillet and with back of spatula, gently press to flatten slightly. Cook for approximately 7 to 10 minutes per side, or until falafels are golden and slightly crispy. Remove to kitchen towel to drain. Repeat with remaining falafels, changing oil between batches.
- To serve, open pita pocket and place lettuce leaf inside.

Place 2 falafels on lettuce and top with Minted Tzatziki and whatever toppings you desire. Wrap tightly and place seam side down on plate.

*Yield: 30 falafels (or enough for dinner for 5, plus leftovers for lunch)*

## Beans, Glorious Beans

In an effort to minimize our intake of saturated fat, Health Canada's Food Guide recommends eating alternatives to meat such as beans, lentils and tofu more often. Not only are plant-based proteins leaner, they also have the added advantage of being less expensive than meat. However the average Canadian continues to consume $2/3$ of a pound of meat per day, and this is 3 times more than the World Cancer Research Fund recommends.[37] Make an effort to eat vegetarian meals more often. Pack soups, salads and sandwiches that contain vegetarian proteins such as legumes, grains and hummus for lunch and prepare more vegetarian dinners.

## Barbecued Asian Salmon

Leftover salmon can be used to make any of the salmon sandwiches or One Pot BC Salade Niçoise (page 128). It can also be packed in a Thermos with whole grain rice, steamed veggies and a drizzle of soy sauce.

½ cup olive oil
¼ cup soy sauce
1 small shallot, finely diced (approximately 1 tbsp)
2 tbsp freshly grated ginger
¼ cup fresh lemon juice
2 tbsp maple syrup
1 piece of wild salmon large enough to provide dinner for your family plus leftovers for the lunch box

- In small bowl, combine olive oil, soy sauce, shallots, ginger, lemon juice and maple syrup. Pour over salmon and let marinate in refrigerator for minimum of 20 minutes and maximum of 4 hours.
- Turn barbecue to high and place salmon flesh side down on grill. Sear for 4 minutes. Turn salmon and place skin side down on grill for 7 to 10 minutes, depending on thickness of your fish. When done, salmon should be moist and opaque throughout and flake easily with fork.

*Yield: Approximately 1 cup of marinade (enough for a large fish)*

## Turkey Sweet Potato Shepherd's Pie

Shepherd's pie is given a healthy twist in this recipe with ground turkey and sweet potato. The combined weight of the potatoes used for the Mashed Potato Topping should be approximately 3 lbs (1½ kg). The amounts given here make 2 pies—1 for dinner tonight and a second for another meal. To send shepherd's pie to school, simply reheat a portion in the microwave and pack it in a preheated Thermos.

3 tbsp olive oil
1 onion, diced
2 carrots, grated
2 stalks celery, diced
12 mushrooms, thinly sliced
2 garlic cloves, minced
1 tbsp chopped fresh sage, or dried
2 tsp dried oregano
2 lbs (1 kg) lean ground turkey
1 can (28 oz /796 mL) diced tomatoes
1 can (5½ oz/156 mL) tomato paste
⅓ cup Homemade Salt-Free Chicken Stock (page 102), or

salt-free or low-sodium canned chicken broth
1 can corn (14 oz/398 mL), drained and rinsed
1 cup frozen peas

Mashed Potato Topping:
3 large baking potatoes, peeled and quartered
1 large sweet potato, peeled and quartered
¼ cup non-hydrogenated margarine
⅓ to ½ cup milk (approximately)

Encore Performances

- Preheat oven to 350°F.
- Heat oil in large, deep skillet or Dutch oven. Add onions, carrots, celery and mushrooms and sauté over medium heat for 10 minutes.
- Add garlic, sage and oregano and stir to combine. Add turkey, breaking it up with spoon, and sauté for 10 minutes.
- Add diced tomatoes, tomato paste, chicken stock, and corn and bring to boil. Reduce heat and simmer for 10 minutes. Add peas and simmer for another 5 minutes.
- Meanwhile prepare Mashed Potato Topping: cook potatoes in boiling water until tender. Drain and mash with margarine and enough milk to achieve a smooth consistency. Evenly divide turkey mixture between 2 8- x 8-inch pans and top with mashed potatoes. Bake in oven for approximately 40 minutes, or until warmed through and bubbling around edges.

*Yield: Each shepherd's pie serves approximately 5 to 6*

## Sharing and Trading Food

Sharing or trading lunches can be a fun and bonding experience. However, we need to address some potential pitfalls. Due to an increase in allergies, some schools prohibit this practice altogether. Regardless, you need to make your child aware of the dangers of sharing food and encourage her to always inquire if friends have allergies before sharing or trading.

Nobody wants their child trading a healthy sandwich for a bag of chips. Appeal to your child's sense of fairness and explain why such a trade is a bad deal. Encourage her to make body-smart choices; trading healthy food for healthy food. If you know that your child likes to trade with a particular friend, approach the parent and together brainstorm ways to make the experience fun and healthy for everyone.

## Udon Noodle Stir-fry

This stir-fry can be made the night before and reheated in the morning, or made fresh while the children eat their breakfast. If you choose to make it in the morning, prep the veggies the night before and store them in the refrigerator overnight.

Because Udon Noodle Stir-fry is so easy to make, it is the perfect last-minute dinner. The recipe can be doubled or even tripled. For a vegetarian version, substitute diced firm tofu for the chicken.

> 2 tbsp soy sauce
> 2 tbsp oyster sauce
> 2 tbsp canola oil
> 1 package (7 oz/200 g) pre-cooked udon noodles
> ½ cup shredded cooked chicken
> 1 cup chopped bok choy
> 1 large carrot, julienned or grated
> 2 large broccoli florets, diced
> 1 green onion, sliced
> 2 tbsp chopped fresh cilantro (optional)

- In small bowl, whisk together soy sauce and oyster sauce; set aside.
- Heat oil in large skillet or wok over medium heat. Add noodles and sauté for 2 minutes.
- Add chicken, bok choy, carrot, broccoli, green onion and soy sauce mixture and sauté for approximately 2 to 3 minutes, or until vegetables are just tender. Remove from heat, add cilantro (if using) and toss.

*Yield: Serves 2*

## Meat in Moderation

Eating meat in moderation is both a healthy choice and an environmentally conscious decision. Meat production is a major contributor to climate change. In fact, the United Nations Food and Agriculture Organization (FAO) estimates that livestock are responsible for 18 % of greenhouse gases, a larger share than the world's transportation sector.[38] It takes approximately 5 to 7 kg of grain to produce 1 kg of beef.[39] Because of the environmental impact of meat-eating, the David Suzuki Foundation recommends that all Canadians increase the number of meat-free meals they eat.

As an alternative to grain-fed or feedlot cattle, consider buying grass-fed beef. It is lower in fat and produces meat with a healthier nutrient profile. Because grass-fed beef doesn't rely on large amounts of fossil fuels to fertilize and transport animal feed, it is also better for the environment. Furthermore, grass-fed cattle live a healthier and more humane existence. While it is true that grass-fed meat is more expensive, it makes sense to eat less meat of a better quality. Both you and the planet will be healthier for it.

# Black Bean Veggie Chili

This chili is made with ground veggie round, which should be available at your local grocery store next to the tofu. If you want to make a beef or turkey chili, simply substitute your preferred meat for the ground veggie round. This chili is designed to appeal to kids and isn't, therefore, terribly spicy. If you want a spicier version, you can always add some extra chili powder while cooking it, or sprinkle a few crushed red-pepper flakes on the adults' portions prior to serving.

¼ cup canola oil
1 onion, diced
¼ cup freshly grated ginger
2 garlic cloves, minced
1 sweet red pepper, seeded and diced
1 sweet yellow pepper, seeded and diced
1½ lb (680 g) ground veggie round
⅓ cup chili powder
3 tbsp ground cumin
½ tsp ground turmeric (optional)
2½ cans (28 oz/796 mL each) diced tomatoes
1 can (5½ oz/156 mL) tomato paste

2 cans (19 oz/540 mL each) black beans, drained and rinsed, or 4 cups cooked black beans
1 can (19 oz/540 mL) white kidney beans, drained and rinsed, or 2 cups cooked white kidney beans
1 can (19 oz/540 mL) red kidney beans, drained and rinsed, or 2 cups cooked red kidney beans
1 can (14 oz/398 mL) corn, drained and rinsed
½ head broccoli, chopped
½ head cauliflower, chopped
3 carrots, thickly sliced
1 bunch fresh cilantro, chopped

Toppings:
1 cup low-fat sour cream, or plain Greek-style yogurt
1 cup shredded Cheddar cheese
1 bunch green onions, sliced

- Heat oil in stockpot over medium heat. Add onions, ginger and garlic and sauté for approximately 5 minutes, or until onions are softened.
- Add red and yellow peppers and sauté for 10 minutes.
- Crumble in ground veggie round and add chili powder, cumin and turmeric (if using). Mix thoroughly and sauté for 5 minutes.
- Add tomatoes, tomato paste and beans. Mix thoroughly and bring to boil. Reduce heat and simmer for 30 minutes with lid mostly on, stirring occasionally.
- Add corn, broccoli, cauliflower and carrots and continue to simmer for 20 minutes. Remove from heat, add cilantro and stir.
- To serve, spoon chili into bowl and top with dollop of sour cream or yogurt and sprinkle of cheese and onions.

*Yield: Serves 10*

## Spanish Omelette

A traditional Spanish omelette, or *tortilla* as it's called in Spain, makes a perfect lunchtime snack. It can be cut into triangles or cubes and eaten as is, or it can be turned into a sandwich as it is in Spain (see recipe for Tortilla Bocadillo on page 52).

This omelette serves 5. If you want to make a bigger one, double the quantities and cook it in a 12-inch skillet—make sure you have a plate or pan large enough to flip the omelette onto. A large saucepan or skillet lid can also be used to flip the omelette.

¼ cup olive oil
1 large baking potato (approximately 1 lb or 500 g), peeled and cut into ½-inch cubes
½ onion, diced
½ tsp kosher salt
5 eggs, lightly beaten

- Heat oil in 8-inch non-stick skillet over medium heat. Add potatoes and sauté for 10 minutes, stirring continually so they don't brown.
- Add onion and salt and sauté for approximately 5 to 10 minutes, or until potatoes are tender but not browned. Transfer potatoes and onions to a plate lined with kitchen towel to drain.
- Return potatoes and onions to skillet and spread evenly to cover surface of pan. Pour eggs on top of potatoes and cook over medium-low heat.
- As edges of omelette begin to cook (after approximately 8 minutes) gently draw them in with rubber spatula to give omelette nice rounded edge. When cooked (approximately 20 minutes in total), egg should be just set, although it is fine if there is a little loose egg on top.
- Wearing oven mitts, flip omelette onto plate. Gently slide omelette back into skillet, uncooked side down, and cook for another 3 minutes. Turn stove off and allow omelette to sit for a few minutes to set. Then flip omelette back onto plate and cut into wedges to serve. It may be eaten hot or chilled.

*Yield: Serves 5*

## Barbecued Asian Flank Steak

When buying a flank steak, be sure to choose one that is large enough to feed your family and provide leftovers for a Flank Steak Sandwich (page 55). If serving a large group, you may need to buy 2 steaks.

¼ cup fresh lime juice
½ tsp lime zest
2 tbsp fish sauce
2 tbsp hoisin sauce

2 tbsp sesame oil

2 tbsp liquid honey

4 garlic cloves, minced

2 tbsp freshly grated ginger

$\frac{1}{3}$ cup chopped fresh cilantro

1 tsp crushed red-pepper flakes

1 flank steak (approximately 2 lbs/1 kg)

- In large bowl, combine lime juice and zest, fish sauce, hoisin sauce, sesame oil, honey, garlic, ginger, cilantro and red-pepper flakes. Pour over steak and let marinate in refrigerator for at least 2 hours or as long as overnight.
- Remove steak from refrigerator 30 minutes before you plan to cook it.
- Turn barbecue to high and, once heated, place steak on grill. Sear for 2 minutes. Reduce heat to medium and turn steak over. Close lid on barbecue and cook for another 7 to 10 minutes, depending on thickness of meat.
- Remove steak from barbecue, tent with foil and let rest for 5 to 10 minutes. Cut steak across grain.

*Yield: Serves 5 to 6*

## Iron Deficiency Linked with a Decline in IQ Scores

An American study demonstrated lower math scores among iron-deficient school-age children.[40] Iron, the essential component of hemoglobin, enables red blood cells to deliver oxygen throughout the body. Without an adequate supply of iron in the diet, the body is unable to manufacture enough red blood cells and this can lead to iron deficiency anemia.

Some symptoms of anemia include fatigue, loss of concentration, brittle nails, paleness, irritability and loss of appetite. If the problem persists, there is a propensity for it to get worse because those who are anemic have a tendency to eat less, thus compounding the problem. Children most at risk include those less than 3 years of age, menstruating teens, extremely picky eaters, dieting teens, vegetarians and those with chronic illness. If you suspect your child may be anemic, consult your doctor, as it can be verified with a simple blood test.

The best way to avoid iron deficiency anemia is to serve a wide variety of iron-rich foods. The body is better able to absorb animal sources of iron. These include beef, pork, turkey, chicken, oysters, tuna, clams and halibut. Good plant-based sources include fortified cereals, dried fruit, legumes, beans and leafy greens. Serving foods that are high in vitamin C, such as oranges and tomatoes, with iron-rich foods will help increase absorption.

## Barbecued Balsamic Chicken

This makes a delicious chicken dinner, and the drumsticks are sure to be appreciated in the next day's lunch box. If 1 chicken isn't enough for your family, buy extra pieces—this recipe makes enough sauce for almost 2 chickens. When barbecuing isn't convenient, you can bake this chicken in the oven.

½ cup ketchup
½ cup balsamic vinegar
2 tbsp honey
2 tbsp grainy mustard
1 tbsp Worcestershire sauce
3 garlic cloves, minced
2 tsp sesame seeds (optional)
1 chicken, cut into pieces (2 thighs, 2 breasts, 2 drumsticks
and wings)

• In small saucepan, combine ketchup, balsamic vinegar,
honey, mustard, Worcestershire sauce and garlic. Bring to
boil, then reduce heat and simmer for 10 minutes, or until

flavours combine. Remove from heat and add sesame seeds. Stir and allow sauce to cool.

- Preheat either outdoor grill or oven to 400°F.
- If barbecuing, place chicken skin side down on grill and cook for about 10 minutes. Turn and cook for another 5 minutes. Brush chicken with barbecue sauce and cook for another 5 to 7 minutes.
- If baking in oven, place chicken skin side up in roasting pan. Bake for approximately 20 minutes. Remove chicken from oven and spoon barbecue sauce over top. Return to oven and bake for another 20 to 25 minutes. When cooked, chicken should be moist and juices will run clear.
- Serve with extra barbecue sauce on the side.

*Yield: Serves 4 to 5*

# 8.

## Baked Goods
## and Desserts

Homemade baked goods are a welcome addition to any lunch box. Not only do home-made cookies, loaves, bars and muffins taste better, they are generally healthier than the average store-bought alternatives. Making your own baked goods enables you to eliminate the unwanted chemical additives found in many commercial varieties and gives you more control over the amount of fat and sugar your children are eating.

A creative chef can always find ways to

improve the nutritional content of recipes. The next time you bake your favourite cookies, try cutting the sugar by ¼ cup. Your kids are likely to be none the wiser. Substituting canola oil for butter in muffins ensures your family will reap the benefits of heart-healthy unsaturated fatty acids. Experiment by substituting ¼ cup of whole wheat flour for white flour when baking. If the difference goes unnoticed, slowly continue to decrease the amount of white flour while increasing the amount of whole wheat flour. Adding seeds, nuts (if your school permits) and dried fruit to baked goods will further improve their nutritional content.

## Lisa's Oatmeal Chocolate Chip Cookies

Packed full of oats and made with whole wheat flour, these cookies are much healthier than your standard chocolate chip cookie. For a yummy twist, add ½ cup of dried cranberries or raisins and ¼ cup of unsweetened coconut to the batter.

| | |
|---|---|
| ¾ cup unsalted butter, softened | ¾ cup whole wheat flour |
| ¾ cup brown sugar | ½ tsp baking soda |
| ½ cup granulated sugar | ½ tsp salt |
| 1 egg, beaten | 1 tsp cinnamon (optional) |
| 2 tbsp water | 2½ cups quick oats |
| 2 tsp pure vanilla extract | 1 rounded cup semi-sweet chocolate chips |

- Preheat oven to 350°F. Grease baking sheets.
- In large bowl, cream butter, brown sugar and granulated sugar together.
- Add egg, water and vanilla and beat until light and fluffy.
- In separate bowl, whisk together whole wheat flour, baking soda, salt, cinnamon (if using) and oats.
- Gently fold wet ingredients into dry. Add chocolate chips and stir to combine.
- Spoon tablespoons of dough 2 inches apart on prepared baking

sheet. Dip fork into water and gently press down to flatten cookies. Bake 12 to 15 minutes, but check after 10 minutes.

- Gently loosen cookies from baking sheet and allow to rest for a few minutes before removing to racks to cool. Cookies can be stored in airtight containers at room temperature or in freezer.

*Yield: 4 dozen cookies*

## Janet's Ginger Sparklers

These cookies are delicious. For a milder flavour, use the lesser amount of spices.

| | |
|---|---|
| ³/₄ cup unsalted butter, softened | 2 tsp baking soda |
| I cup brown sugar | ½ tsp salt |
| ¼ cup molasses | I to I ½ tsp ground ginger |
| I egg | I to I ½tsp ground cinnamon |
| I cup all-purpose white flour | ½ to ³/₄ tsp ground cloves |
| I cup whole wheat flour | Granulated sugar for rolling |

- Preheat oven to 375°F. Grease baking sheets.
- In large bowl, cream together butter, brown sugar, molasses and egg until light and fluffy.
- In separate bowl, whisk together all-purpose flour, whole wheat flour, baking soda, salt, ginger, cinnamon and cloves. Add to butter mixture and stir just until blended.
- Roll teaspoons of dough into balls and roll in granulated sugar. Place on prepared baking sheet and bake for 8 to 10 minutes. Let cookies cool 2 minutes before transferring to racks to cool completely.

*Yield: Approximately 5 dozen*

# Birdseed Cookies

I cup whole wheat flour
I tsp baking powder
I tsp baking soda
³⁄₄ cup rolled oats
¹⁄₄ cup unsweetened shredded coconut
¹⁄₂ cup raisins
³⁄₄ cup unsalted sunflower seeds
¹⁄₄ cup sesame seeds
¹⁄₂ cup ground flax seeds
I cup dark chocolate chips
¹⁄₂ cup unsalted butter, softened
¹⁄₂ cup packed brown sugar
2 eggs
I tsp pure vanilla extract

- Preheat oven to 350°F.
- In large bowl, whisk together flour, baking powder and baking soda.
- Add oats, coconut, raisins, sunflower seeds, sesame seeds, ground flax seeds and chocolate chips and stir to combine.
- In separate bowl, cream together butter and brown sugar. Add eggs and vanilla and beat until light and fluffy.
- Add flour mixture 1 cup at a time and stir until combined.
- Spoon tablespoons of dough 2 inches apart on ungreased baking sheet.
- Dip fork into water and gently press down to flatten cookie. Bake for 10 to 12 minutes. Let cookies cool 2 minutes before transferring to racks to cool completely.

*Yield: Approximately 4 dozen*

## Seeds of Inspiration

Given that seeds are the source of life for new plants, it is not surprising that they are nutrient dense. Like nuts, seeds are a good source of protein, heart healthy polyunsaturated fatty acids, vitamins, minerals and fibre. Sesame seeds are a good non-dairy source of calcium, while flaxseeds contain omega-3 fatty acids. Pumpkin seeds are rich in immune-boosting zinc, whereas sunflower seeds are one of the best sources of vitamin E. Vitamin E acts as a powerful antioxidant protecting cells from the damaging effects of free radicals.

Given that many schools are "nut-free" and that seeds contain many of the same nutrients, it only makes sense to substitute seeds for nuts. They are just the thing to snack on and can be used instead of nuts in both baking and trail mixes. Furthermore, seed butters are an ideal alternative to nut butters, making nutritious and appealing sandwiches. Seed butters are becoming increasingly common and are available in many stores across Canada.

## No Bake Chocolate Haystacks

Because they are so easy to make, Chocolate Haystacks are the perfect first foray into desserts. Pretty soon your kids will be making them on their own.

2 cups granulated sugar
1/2 cup milk
1/2 cup butter
5 tbsp cocoa
1/2 tsp salt
1 tsp pure vanilla extract
3 cups quick oats
1 cup unsweetened coconut

• Line 2 baking sheets with parchment paper or waxed paper.
• In saucepan, combine sugar, milk, butter, cocoa, salt and vanilla. Place over medium heat and bring to boil. Remove

from heat.
- Add oats and coconut and stir to combine. Let cool for a few minutes.
- Drop by tablespoonfuls onto prepared baking sheets and refrigerate for 1 to 2 hours.

*Yield: Approximately 4 dozen cookies*

## Orange Craze Muffins

These muffins are also delicious with dates instead of cranberries.

| | |
|---|---|
| 1 orange, unpeeled and washed | 1 tsp baking powder |
| ½ cup orange juice | 1 tsp baking soda |
| 1 egg or 2 egg whites | ½ tsp salt |
| ¼ cup canola oil | ½ cup granulated sugar |
| 1 cup all-purpose white flour | ½ cup whole wheat flour |
| | ¾ cup dried cranberries |

- Preheat oven to 375°F. Grease 12-cup muffin tin.
- Cut orange (peel and all) into 8 pieces and place in bowl of food processor.
- Add orange juice, egg and oil and process until smooth.
- In separate bowl, sift together flour, baking powder, baking soda and salt. Add sugar and whole wheat flour and whisk to combine.
- Gently fold orange mixture into flour mixture. Fold in cranberries. Do not overmix.
- Spoon batter into prepared muffin cups and bake for 15 to 20 minutes. When done, muffins will be puffed and toothpick inserted into centre will come out clean. Let muffins cool in pan on wire rack for 5 minutes before turning them out on rack to cool completely.

*Yield: 12 muffins*

## Portion Sizes

In North America, portion sizes seem to be expanding with our waist-lines, and this increase is thought to be contributing to our childhood obesity epidemic. There is nothing wrong with packing a little dessert to finish off a healthy lunch. But what you don't want is your child filling up on a gigantic cookie or a big piece of chocolate cake instead of eating her sandwich. Many store-bought cookies are 4 to 5 times the size of the average homemade cookie. Help your child understand what is reasonable by packing sensible portions. As a general rule, a tablespoon of dough makes the perfect-sized cookie and, if buying store-bought baked goods, consider cutting portions into halves or quarters. The next time you make muffins, consider using a mini-muffin pan and cut the baking time by about half. When done, muffins will be puffed and a toothpick inserted into the centre should come out clean.

## Mini Banana Chocolate Chip Muffins

Mini muffins are the perfect size for a lunch box treat.

¾ cup all-purpose white
   flour
1 tsp baking powder
1 tsp baking soda
½ tsp salt
¾ cup whole wheat flour
⅓ cup wheat germ
½ tsp cinnamon

½ tsp ground nutmeg
½ cup chocolate chips
1 large egg, beaten
3 mashed ripe bananas
   (approximately 1 cup)
½ cup packed brown sugar
½ cup canola oil
1 tsp pure vanilla extract

- Preheat oven to 400°F. Grease 24-cup mini-muffin tin.
- In large bowl, sift together all-purpose flour, baking powder, baking soda and salt. Add whole wheat flour, wheat germ, cinnamon, nutmeg and chocolate chips and stir to combine.
- In another bowl, combine egg, mashed bananas, brown sugar, canola oil and vanilla. Gently fold banana mixture into flour mixture. Do not overmix.

- Spoon batter into prepared muffin tin. Bake for 10 to 15
minutes, checking after 10 minutes. When done, muffins
will be puffed and toothpick inserted into centre will come
out clean. Let muffins cool in pan on wire rack for 5
minutes before turning them out on rack to cool
completely.

*Yield: 24 mini muffins*

## Banana Chunk Bran Muffins

This recipe makes a fairly large quantity. Extra muffins can be
stored in the freezer.

| | |
|---|---|
| 2 cups wheat bran | 2 cups all-purpose white |
| 2 cups buttermilk | flour |
| 1/2 cup canola oil | 1 cup whole wheat flour |
| 1/2 cup brown sugar | 1 1/2 tsp baking powder |
| 2/3 cup molasses | 1/2 tsp baking soda |
| 4 large eggs | 1 tsp salt |
| 1 tsp pure vanilla extract | 2 cups raisins |
| Zest from 1 orange | 2 cups diced bananas |
| (approximately 2 tsp) | (approximately 2 large or |
| | 3 medium bananas) |

- Preheat oven to 350°F. Grease 2 12-cup muffin tins.
- In small bowl, combine bran and buttermilk and set aside.
- In large bowl, combine oil, brown sugar, molasses, eggs,
vanilla and orange zest. Add bran mixture to oil mixture
and combine.
- In separate bowl, whisk together all-purpose flour, whole
wheat flour, baking powder, baking soda and salt. Gently
fold bran mixture into flour mixture. Fold in raisins and
bananas. Do not overmix.

- Spoon batter into prepared muffin tins and bake 25 to 30 minutes. (Bake mini muffins for approximately 15 minutes.) When done, muffins will be puffed and toothpick inserted into centre will come out clean. Let muffins cool in pan on wire rack for 5 minutes before turning them out on rack to cool completely.

*Yield: 24 muffins*

## Banana Bread

Made with whole wheat flour and just a touch of canola oil, this recipe is a bit healthier than the average banana bread.

| | |
|---|---|
| ¾ cup all-purpose white flour | 1 egg |
| ¾ cup whole wheat flour | ⅓ cup granulated sugar |
| 1 tsp baking soda | 2 tbsp canola oil |
| ½ tsp baking powder | 3 large ripe bananas, |
| ½ tsp salt | mashed |
| | ¼ cup milk |

- Preheat oven to 350°F. Grease 9- x 5-inch loaf pan.
- In bowl, whisk together all-purpose flour, whole wheat flour, baking soda, baking powder and salt.
- In separate large bowl, beat egg, sugar and canola oil until combined. Add bananas and milk and stir to combine.
- Gently fold flour mixture into banana mixture until just moistened. Pour into prepared pan and bake for 45 minutes, or until skewer inserted in centre of loaf comes out clean.

*Yield: 1 9- x 5-inch loaf*

# Blueberry Coffee Cake

¼ cup butter, softened
¾ cup granulated sugar
1 egg
½ cup milk
1 cup whole wheat flour
1 cup all-purpose white flour
2 tsp baking powder
½ tsp salt
2 cups blueberries

Streusel Topping:
½ cup granulated sugar
⅓ cup all-purpose white flour
1½ tsp cinnamon
¼ cup butter, slightly softened

- Preheat oven to 375°F. Grease 9- x 9-inch pan.
- In large bowl, beat together butter, sugar and egg until light and fluffy. Beat in milk.
- In separate bowl, whisk together whole wheat flour, white flour, baking powder and salt. Gently fold into milk mixture. Fold in blueberries. Pour batter into prepared pan.
- For Streusel Topping: In small bowl, combine sugar, flour and cinnamon. With a fork or pastry cutter, cut in butter until pea-sized clumps form. Spread over cake batter.
- Bake for 45 to 50 minutes or until skewer inserted into centre comes out clean.

*Yield: 1 9- x 9-inch cake*

## Gayle's Homemade Granola Bars

Having experimented with more granola bar recipes than we care to count, these are the best, hands down! Making your own granola bars enables you to eliminate the unwanted additives and high sugar content of many packaged granola bars. These are made with almond butter, so if your child is attending a nut-free school, substitute sunflower seed butter or soy butter for excellent results.

3 cups rolled oats
1/2 cup flax seeds
1 cup sunflower seeds
1 cup crispy rice cereal (try to find a whole grain one, but
   Rice Krispies will do in a pinch)
1 cup dried cranberries
1/2 cup diced dates or raisins
1/2 cup unsweetened shredded coconut
1/2 cup honey
1 cup almond butter
1 tsp pure vanilla extract
1/2 tsp cinnamon
1/2 tsp salt
2 large eggs, beaten
1/2 cup chocolate chips (optional)

- Preheat oven to 350°F. Grease 9- x 13-inch pan and line with parchment paper, leaving ends lying over edges of pan. (This will allow you to lift granola bars out of pan with ease.)
- Spread oats, flax seeds and sunflower seeds on baking sheet and toast in oven for 8 minutes. Remove from oven and stir. Return to oven and toast for another 8 minutes. Place in large bowl.
- Add rice cereal, cranberries, dates and coconut to toasted oat mixture and stir to combine.
- In saucepan, combine honey, almond butter, vanilla, cinnamon and salt. Place over medium heat and stir for

approximately 5 to 7 minutes. Add to oat mixture and stir to combine. Let cool.

- Add eggs and stir to combine. Spread granola mixture in pan, pressing with back of spoon to smooth it out. Sprinkle with chocolate chips (if using) and press into granola.
- Bake for 20 to 25 minutes or until granola is golden brown. Let cool in pan for 25 minutes. Cut into bars and place pan in refrigerator for 30 minutes. Break apart bars and store in refrigerator until ready to be eaten.

*Yield: 24 bars*

### Granola Bars

Many commercial granola bars are little better than chocolate bars. If you do not have time to make homemade granola bars, use the Nutrition Facts table on the package to help you choose the healthiest possible bars. These bars will have the highest percentage daily value (% DV) of fibre, while containing the least amount of sugar and the lowest % DV for both sodium and saturated fat. And be sure to avoid any packaged foods that contain added trans fats.

## Ashley's Date Squares

Named after Cheryl's daughter, this yummy treat is one of Ashley's favourites.

| | |
|---|---|
| 1 package (1 lb or 500 g) pitted dates, chopped | 1¼ cup quick oats |
| 1 cup water | 1 cup brown sugar |
| 2 tsp lemon juice | 1 tsp baking soda |
| 1½ cups whole wheat flour | ¼ tsp salt |
| | ¾ cup unsalted butter, melted |

- Preheat oven to 350°F.
- In small saucepan, add dates, water, and lemon juice. Place over medium-high heat and bring to boil. Reduce heat and simmer for approximately 5 to 10 minutes, or until dates are soft. Remove from heat and set aside.
- In large bowl, combine flour, oats, sugar, baking soda and salt. Add melted butter and combine.
- Press half of oat mixture in bottom of ungreased 9- x 9-inch pan. Evenly spread date mixture on top and sprinkle with remaining oat mixture. Bake for 30 minutes or until golden brown.
- Cool for 10 minutes, then cut into squares. Allow to cool thoroughly before serving

*Yield: 1 9- x 9-inch pan, approximately 16 squares*

## Packing for Success!

A recent Canadian study indicated that diet quality affects academic performance.[41] The findings are crucial, given that academic performance has a significant impact on future educational attainment, income, quality of life and health. Packing a healthy lunch is just one of the many ways you can set your children up for success.

## Chelsea's Carrot Squares

Named after Cheryl's daughter, these squares are a welcome lunch box treat.

1 ½ cups all-purpose white flour
¾ tsp baking soda
1 ½ tsp cinnamon
1 tsp salt

¾ cup granulated sugar
½ cup plus 1 tbsp canola oil
2 eggs
1 ½ cups grated carrots

Orange Icing:

1/4 cup butter, softened                 1 3/4 cups icing sugar

2 1/2 tbsp orange juice

- Preheat oven to 350°F. Grease 9- x 9-inch baking pan.
- In large bowl, whisk together flour, baking soda, cinnamon and salt until combined.
- In small bowl combine sugar, oil, eggs and carrots. Fold into flour mixture until just combined. Pour into prepared pan. Bake for 30 to 40 minutes or until toothpick inserted into centre comes out clean. Let cool completely.
- For Orange Icing: Cream butter and orange juice together. Gradually beat in icing sugar until combined. Spread evenly over cooled cake. Cut into squares.

*Yield: 1 9- x 9-inch cake*

## Cinnamon Loaf

This simple loaf makes an easy, delicious addition to any brunch, and leftovers (if there are any) can be packed with lunch the next day.

1/2 cup butter, softened            1 tsp baking powder

1 cup granulated sugar             1/2 tsp baking soda

2 eggs                                     Dash of salt

1 cup light sour cream

2 tsp pure vanilla extract         Cinnamon Mixture:

1 1/2 cups all-purpose white      3 tbsp brown sugar

   flour                                    1 1/2 tbsp cinnamon

1/2 cup whole wheat flour

- Preheat oven to 350°F. Grease 9- x 5-inch loaf pan.
- In large bowl, cream butter and sugar together. Add eggs, sour cream and vanilla and beat until combined.

- In separate bowl, whisk together all-purpose flour, whole wheat flour, baking powder, baking soda and salt. Fold into sour cream mixture just until combined. Do not overmix. Spread half of batter in prepared pan.
- For Cinnamon Mixture: In small bowl, combine brown sugar and cinnamon. Spread over batter in pan. Spread remaining batter over top and then swirl a knife through the 3 layers. Bake for 45 to 50 minutes or until toothpick inserted into centre of loaf comes out clean.

*Yield: 1 9- x 5-inch loaf*

9.

After-School
Snacks

It is good practice to offer all children fruit and vegetables for snacks and to limit processed foods as much as possible. Often children are famished when they come home from school. Make the most of this opportunity to add another serving of Vegetables and Fruit to your child's diet. Set out a platter of veggies with an enticing dip (page 96) or make homemade fruit-filled popsicles (page 187). Always a hit, homemade popsicles are a tantalizing way to boost your child's fruit consumption.

A healthy snack should include foods from at least 2 of the 4 food groups. For instance, frosty fruit smoothies (page 185) made with fruit and yogurt are ideal. As an added benefit, they contain the 2 food groups commonly deficient in the diets of many Canadian children. If you cannot send peanut butter to school, offer it as part of a nutritious snack. Peanut butter, or any other nut butter, is high in protein and a good source of both fibre and heart-healthy unsaturated fatty acids. Peanut butter can be served with whole grain breads and crackers, as well as fruit. For a change, spread peanut butter on either a slice of apple or a piece of banana.

Instead of offering a platter of cookies, set out a single cookie with a sliced apple or some berries and serve a glass of milk alongside. When buying packaged foods, read ingredient lists and compare Nutrition Facts tables to help you buy those that are higher in fibre, are lower in sodium, fat and sugar, and contain minimal or no chemical additives. When buying munchies, opt for baked over fried and offer air-popped popcorn. Popcorn, a whole grain, is high in fibre and very filling, making it the perfect snack for the insatiable teen.

Teenagers and those coming home to empty houses will make their own snacks. Before this happens, it's important that you set some ground rules, since nobody wants to come home to discover a crucial ingredient for dinner is missing or that the baking cupboard has been raided of chocolate chips. Talk to your kids about what constitutes a healthy snack and point out the cupboards and drawers they are welcome to, as well as those that are off limits. Use the chart on page 13 to organize your kitchen so that all 4 food groups are represented and accessible.

# Smoothies

If your child has a milk allergy or is lactose intolerant, soy milk can be substituted in any of the following recipes.

## Strawberry Banana Smoothie

This can be made with any type of berries. Try substituting frozen blueberries, raspberries or mixed berries for the strawberries.

I cup milk
½ cup plain yogurt
I banana
I ½ cups frozen strawberries

• Combine ingredients in a blender and blend until smooth.

*Yield: Serves 2 to 3*

## Mixed Berry Smoothie

I ½ cups frozen mixed berries
I ½ cups orange juice

• Combine ingredients in a blender and blend until smooth.

*Yield: Serves 2 to 3*

TIP: When bananas begin to brown, put them in the freezer to be used for baking or smoothies.

# Chocolate Banana Tofu Shake

**2 frozen bananas**
**1 ½ cups chocolate milk**
**½ cup silken tofu**

- Briefly run frozen bananas under warm water to loosen skin. Then peel banana with paring knife.
- Combine ingredients in blender and blend until smooth.

*Yield: Serves 4*

# Banana Milkshake

Try making this without the honey first, since there's no point in encouraging a sweet tooth. If your child isn't so fond of it, add the honey the next time you make it.

**2 frozen bananas**
**1 ½ cups milk**
**½ cup plain yogurt**
**Approximately 1 tsp of honey (optional)**

- Briefly run frozen bananas under warm water to loosen skin. Then peel banana with paring knife.
- Combine ingredients in blender and blend until smooth.

*Yield: Serves 2 to 3*

# Popsicles

Made with fresh or frozen fruit, homemade popsicles are wonderful after-school snacks. They are a much healthier alternative to the sugar-laden, store-bought varieties. If you choose to add sugar or honey, stir in just enough to sweeten the fruit. For the following recipes, you will need plastic Popsicle moulds.

## Strawberry Creamsicles

5 cups fresh or frozen strawberries
½ cup Greek-style plain yogurt (above 3% milk fat)
½ cup milk
I tbsp honey (approximately)

- If using frozen berries, defrost them.
- In bowl of food processor, place strawberries and process until puréed.
- Strain strawberries through fine sieve to remove seeds. You should have approximately 1¼ cups strawberry purée.
- Place strawberry purée back in bowl of food processor and add yogurt and milk. Process until combined. Add just enough honey to sweeten fruit and process until combined. Pour into Popsicle moulds and freeze.

*Yield: Approximately 8 to 10 Popsicles, depending on size of moulds*

## A Word to the Wise

The consumption of soda pop has been linked to obesity, tooth decay, osteoporosis and pancreatic cancer—one of the most lethal forms of the disease. A recent large-scale study indicated that people who consumed as little as 2 or more sugar-sweetened soft drinks per week had an 85 per cent increased risk of developing pancreatic cancer, compared with those who did not.[42] For children these problems are exacerbated by the fact that soda pop consumption tends to rise during the teenage years. It is estimated that the average teen gets approximately 13 per cent of his daily calories from soda pop.[43] Don't let your children drink this much pop. Keep it out of the lunch box and talk to them about the problems associated with soft drinks.

# Raspberry Orange Popsicles

5 cups fresh or frozen raspberries
1 cup orange juice
1 tbsp honey (approximately)

- If using frozen berries, defrost them.
- In bowl of food processor, place raspberries and process until puréed.
- Strain raspberries through fine sieve to remove seeds.
- Place raspberry purée back in bowl of food processor and add orange juice. Purée until smooth.
- Add just enough honey to sweeten the fruit and process until combined. Pour into Popsicle moulds and freeze.

*Yield: Approximately 8 to10 Popsicles, depending on size of moulds*

## Moderation is the Key

There is nothing wrong with adding a little treat to your child's lunch box. If all goodies were eliminated, children would be more likely to overindulge when given the chance. We need to move away from the idea of "good foods" and "bad foods." Instead, teach your children to think in terms of "everyday foods" (whole grains, fruit, vegetables, lean protein and low-fat dairy products) and "sometimes foods" (chips, candy and fast food). If, for occasional variety, you add a chocolate bar to your child's lunch box, opt for the 2-bite bar instead of the larger one. Remember, healthy eating is the sum of all food choices over time, and any food, when eaten in moderation, can be part of a healthy diet.

## Chocolate Covered Frozen Bananas

Chocolate Covered Frozen Bananas can be eaten as popsicles or bite-sized frozen treats. To make a frozen banana Popsicle you will need wooden Popsicle sticks (or flat wooden craft sticks).

2 cups peanuts or pecans, finely chopped
2 cups unsweetened shredded coconut
2 1/2 cups dark chocolate chips
4 to 5 bananas (depending on size)
4 to 5 flat wooden craft sticks (optional)

- Line baking sheet with parchment paper. In one bowl place peanuts and in second bowl place coconut.
- If making frozen banana Popsicles, gently insert wooden stick into one end of each banana.
- In top of double boiler over hot (not boiling) water, melt chocolate. Dip each banana in chocolate, gently turning until well coated, then roll in either nuts or coconut and place on prepared baking sheet.
- Freeze bananas solid.
- Frozen banana popsicles can be stored in the freezer until ready to eat.

- If making bite-sized frozen banana treats, remove bananas from freezer. With a sharp knife cut into 1-inch slices. Store in freezer until ready to eat.

*Yield: Serves 5 to 6*

Appendix I:

Sample Meal
Planners

The following sample meal planners are designed to guide you in planning your children's lunches. Each of the following lunches contains foods from all 4 food groups and includes at least 2 servings of Vegetables and Fruit, as well as 2 servings of Grain Products. The lunches within each week offer a daily variety of different foods—a healthy diet is a varied diet! Planning a week's worth of lunches in advance and shopping accordingly increases the odds of your children eating healthily.

Friday's lunches are designed as sample meals for young children or those with small appetites. When dealing with these kids it's crucial you keep portions small so they don't become overwhelmed. If you pack a whole apple and your child only eats a few slices, adjust the lunch accordingly. This simple step helps to reduce food waste and ensures lunch is a more positive experience for everyone. After all, there is nothing like success to bolster confidence.

# WEEK ONE

### MONDAY

Beef Barley Soup, 2 Wasa whole grain crackers, 2 slices of low-fat cheese, Fruit Pot with mandarin orange segments and blueberries and water

### TUESDAY

Dilly Delicious Tuna Pita Pocket, carrots and strips of sweet red pepper with Dilly Delicious Dip, Gayle's Homemade Granola Bar and milk

### WEDNESDAY

The Greek Picnic, Yogurt Pot with frozen blueberries and a drizzle of honey, Lisa's Oatmeal Chocolate Chip Cookie and 100% pure fruit juice

### THURSDAY

Black Bean Turkey Taco Wrap, assorted vegetable sticks with Roasted Red Pepper and Basil Hummus, a pear, Ashley's Date Square and milk

### FRIDAY

4 Salmon Salad Pinwheels, a few carrot sticks with Minted Tzatziki, 1 Fruit Filled Jell-O Finger and water

# WEEK TWO

### MONDAY

Kid's Pesto Pasta Salad, Edamame, apple slices with yogurt for dipping and water

### TUESDAY

Salmon Souvlaki Pita, cucumber sticks and cherry tomatoes with Homemade Hummus, Janet's Ginger Sparkler and milk

### WEDNESDAY

One Pot Kid's Cobb Salad, whole grain crackers, Yogurt Pot with diced mango and a drizzle of honey, water and Ashley's Date Square

### THURSDAY

Roasted Tomato Lentil Soup, whole grain roll, 2 slices of Cheddar cheese, Fruit Pot with strawberries and cubes of cantaloupe and water

### FRIDAY

The Ploughman's Lunch, a few apple slices and 100% pure fruit juice

# WEEK THREE

**MONDAY**

Ellie's Lunch Box Pizzas, air-popped popcorn, assorted vegetable sticks with Roasted Red Pepper and Basil Hummus and 100% pure fruit juice

**TUESDAY**

Mexican Black Bean Soup with Chicken, 2 slices of whole grain bread, carrot sticks, Yogurt Pot with diced strawberries and a drizzle of honey and water

**WEDNESDAY**

Middle Eastern Picnic, Blueberry Coffee Cake and milk

**THURSDAY**

Salade Niçoise, Yogurt Pot with frozen raspberries and a drizzle of honey, Gayle's Homemade Granola Bar and water

**FRIDAY**

Devilled Eggs, whole grain rice crackers, a chunk of Cheddar cheese, a few grapes, a couple of slices of apple and milk

# WEEK FOUR

**MONDAY**

Curried Chickpea and Vegetable Soup, whole grain roll with a few slices of low-fat cheese, cherries, Chocolate Haystacks and water

**TUESDAY**

Karen's Greek Quinoa Salad, Toasted Whole Wheat Pita Chips with Homemade Hummus and vegetable sticks, Gayle's Homemade Granola Bar and milk

**WEDNESDAY**

Veggie Hummus Wrap, Yogurt Pot with assorted berries and a drizzle of honey, air-popped popcorn, Cheryl's Birdseed Cookies and water

**THURSDAY**

Salmon Salad Bunwich with Caper Dill Mayonnaise, Cheese Stuffed Celery, Fruit Pot with kiwi slices and strawberries and water

**FRIDAY**

Chicken Noodle Soup, slice of whole grain bread, Lisa's Oatmeal Chocolate Chip Cookie and milk

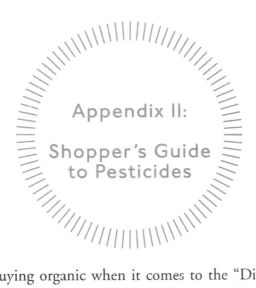

# Appendix II:

## Shopper's Guide to Pesticides

Consider buying organic when it comes to the "Dirty Dozen," to avoid the produce that has the highest possible exposure to pesticide residues.

| DIRTY DOZEN | CLEAN 15 |
|---|---|
| (Highest in Pesticides) | (Lowest in Pesticides) |
| (Starting with the worst) | (Starting with the best) |
| Celery | Onions |
| Peaches | Avocados |
| Strawberries | Sweet Corn |
| Apples | Pineapple |
| Blueberries* | Mangoes |
| Nectarines | Sweet Peas |
| Bell Peppers | Asparagus |
| Spinach | Kiwi |
| Cherries | Cabbage |
| Kale/Collard Greens | Eggplant |
| Potatoes | Cantaloupe* |
| Grapes (imported) | Watermelon |
| | Grapefruit |
| | Sweet Potato |
| | Honeydew |
| * U.S. domestic varieties only | Melon |

Source: Environmental Working Group © 2010. Reprinted with permission. www.foodnews.org

Appendix III:

Resources

## Websites

**American Academy of Allergy Asthma & Immunology**

www.aaai.org

**American Dietetic Association**

www.eatright.org

**American Academy of Pediatrics**

www.aap.org

**Anemia Institute for Research & Education**

www.optimizinghealth.org

**Authors' Website**

www.goodfoodbooksforkids.com

**HealthLink BC**

www.healthlinkbc.ca

British Columbia Medical Association
www.bcma.org

Canadian Food Inspection Agency
www.inspection.gc.ca

Canadian Paediatric Society
www.cps.ca

Canada's Physical Activity Guide to Healthy Active Living
http://www.phac-aspc.gc.ca/hp-ps/hl-mvs/
pa-ap/index-eng.php

Centers for Disease Control and Prevention BMI Percentile
Calculator for Child and Teen
http://apps.nccd.cdc.gov/dnpabmi/Calculator.aspx

Childhood Obesity Foundation
http://www.childhoodobesityfoundation.ca/

Dietitian Services at Healthlink B.C.
www.healthlinkbc.ca/dietitian/

David Suzuki Foundation
www.davidsuzuki.org

Dietitians of Canada
www.dietitians.ca/eatwell

Eating Well with Canada's Food Guide
www.hc-sc.gc.ca/fn-an/food-guide-aliment/index-eng.php

Eating Well with Canada's Food Guide: First Nations,
Inuit and Métis
www.hc-sc.gc.ca/fn-an/pubs/fnim-pnim/index-eng.php

Eisler for Kids
www.eislerforkids.com

Environmental Working Group
www.ewg.org

Farmer's Markets Canada
www.farmersmarketscanada.ca

Health Canada
www.hc-sc.gc.ca

Lesliebeck.com
www.lesliebeck.com

Vancouver Farmers Markets
www.eatlocal.org

## Books

Bradshaw, B., & Bramley, L.D. (2004). *The Baby's Table*. Toronto, ON: Random House Canada.

Bradshaw, B., & Mutch, C. (2008). *The Good Food Book For Families*. Toronto, ON: Random House Canada.

Laumann, S. (2006). *Child's Play*. Toronto, ON: Random House Canada.

Satter, E. (1987). *How to Get Your Kid to Eat . . . But Not Too Much*. Boulder, CO: Bull Publishing Company.

Waverman, E. & Mott, E. (2007). *Whining & Dining*. Toronto, ON: Random House Canada.

Friedman, J. & Saunders, N. (2007). *Canada's Baby Care Book*. Toronto, ON: Robert Rose Inc.

Friedman, J. (2009). *Canada's Toddler Care Book*. Toronto, ON: Robert Rose Inc.

# Acknowledgements

We would like to thank a number of people whose help and support contributed greatly to this book. Dan Kalla, Nancy Stairs and Val Bradshaw, we thank you for generously sharing your editorial expertise with us. We thank Dr. Jeremy Friedman for his kind and thoughtful words. To our copy editor, Stacey Cameron, we thank you for dotting our i's and crossing our t's. We thank our publisher, Random House Canada, for believing in the importance of our message and helping to bring this book to fruition. To our editor, Pamela Murray, you are a pleasure to work with and we appreciate your knowledge and experience.

In addition, we would like to thank all those who tested, tasted, retested, inspired or donated recipes. They are: Shaughn Mohammed, Julia Rudd, Lisa Hudson, Mike Hudson, Tamara Vrooman, Karen Fryer, Cathy Radcliffe, Gayle McLeod, Janet Mutch, Dan Kalla, Diane Petter, Craig Bramley, Val Bradshaw, Dick Bradshaw, Ines Eisses, Jeff Petter, Shannon Ferguson, Christina Shearer and James Schaeffer. A special thanks goes to Daphne Hodgins, recipe tester extraordinaire. We are grateful for your honest feedback and willingness to test absolutely any recipe. Thanks to our wonderful children, Charlie, Chelsea, Ashley and Elliotte, for allowing us to practise what we preach. Your lunch box critiques were an inspiration. To our husbands, Dan and Jeff, we are thankful for your technical expertise, but more importantly, for your love and emotional support.

# Notes

1. Statistics Canada, "Overview of Canadians' Eating Habits," The Daily, http://www.statcan.gc.ca/daily-quotidien/060706/dq060706b-eng.htm.

2. C. J. Reissig et al., "Caffeinated Energy Drinks—A Growing Problem," *Drug and Alcohol Dependence* 99 (2009): 1–10.

3. N. MacDonald et al., "Caffeinating Children and Youth," *Canadian Medical Association Journal,* Editorial, Early Release, (2010).

4. Statistics Canada, "Canadian Health Measures Survey: Lead, Bisphenol A and Mercury," The Daily, http://www.statcan.gc.ca/daily-quotidien/100816/dq100816a-eng.htm (accessed September 16, 2010).

5. Mai A. Elobeid et al., "Putative Environmental-Endocrine Disruptors and Obesity: A Review," *Current Opinion in Endocrinology, Diabetes and Obesity* 15 (2008): 403–08.

6. Shuk-Mei Ho et al., "Developmental Exposure to

Estradiol and Bisphenol A Increases Susceptibility to Prostate Carcinogenesis and Epigenetically Regulates Phosphodiesterase Type 4 Variant 4," *Cancer Research* 66 (2006): 5624–32.

7.  Milena Durando et al., "Prenatal Bisphenol A Exposure Induces Preneoplastic Lesions in the Mammary Gland in Wistar Rats," *Environmental Health Perspectives* 115 (2007): 80–86.

8.  Maricel V. Maffini et al., "Endocrine Disruptors and Reproductive Health: The Case of Bisphenol A," *Molecular and Cellular Endocrinology* 265–255 (2006): 179–86.

9.  Health Canada, "Health Canada Responds to Concerns Raised about Bisphenol A in Canned Food," Information Update, http://www.hc-sc.gc.ca/ahc-asc/media/nr-cp/_2008/2008_84-eng.php (accessed September 16, 2010).

10. Childhood Obesity Foundation, "Statistics," http://www.childhoodobesityfoundation.ca/statistics (accessed September 16, 2010).

11. Health Canada, "Family Guide to Physical Activity for Children (6 to 9 years of age)," http://www.phac-aspc.gc.ca/hp-ps/hl-mvs/pag-gap/cy-ej/children-enfants/index-eng.php (accessed September 16, 2010).

12. Statistics Canada, "Overview of Canadians' Eating Habits," The Daily, http://www.statcan.gc.ca/daily-quotidien/060706/dq060706b-eng.htm.

13. Kate Sherwood, "Leafy Greens," *Nutrition Action,* May 2010.

14. Health Canada, "Do Canadian Adolescents Meet Their

Nutrient Requirements through Food Intake Alone?" Food and Nutrition, http://www.hc-sc.gc.ca/fn-an/surveill/nutrition/commun/art-nutr-adol-eng.php (accessed September 16, 2010).

15. M. Maynard et al., "Fruit, Vegetables, and Antioxidants in Childhood and Risk of Adult Cancer: the Boyd Orr Cohort," *Journal of Epidemiology and Community Health* 61 (2007): 218–25.

16. Joanne Slavin, "Whole Grains and Human Health," *Nutrition Research Reviews* 17 (2004): 99–110.

17. Health Canada, "Health Canada Advises Specific Groups to Limit Their Consumption of Canned Albacore Tuna," About Health Canada, http://www.hc-sc.gc.ca/ahc-asc/media/advisories-avis/_2007/2007_14-eng.php (accessed September 16, 2010).

18. Public Health Agency of Canada, "Update to 2008 Listeria Monocytogenes Case Numbers," Food Safety, http://www.phac-aspc.gc.ca/alert-alerte/listeria/listeria_20100413-eng.php (accessed September 17, 2010).

19. Kentaro Murakami et al., "Fish and n-3 Polyunsaturated Fatty Acid Intake and Depressive Symptoms: Ryukyus Child Health Study," *Pediatrics,* 126, no. 3 (2010), http://pediatrics.aappublications.org/cgi/content/abstract/126/3/e623 (accessed September 17, 2010).

20. Health Canada, "Questions and Answers—Hormonal Growth Promoters," Drug and Health Products, http://www.hc-sc.gc.ca/dhp-mps/vet/faq/growth_hormones_promoters_croissance_hormonaux_stimulateurs-eng.php (accessed September 17, 2010).

21. Jaimie N. Davis et al., "Inverse Relation between Dietary Fibre Intake and Visceral Adiposity in Overweight Latino Youth," *The American Journal of Clinical Nutrition* 90 (2009): 1160–66.

22. D. E. Roth et al., "Are National Vitamin D Guidelines Sufficient to Maintain Adequate Blood Levels in Children?" *Canadian Journal of Public Health* 96 (2005): 443–49.

23. Health Canada, "Vitamin D and Calcium: Updated Dietary Reference Intakes," Food and Nutrition, http://www.hc-sc.gc.ca/fn-an/nutrition/vitamin/vita-d-eng.php (accessed December 1, 2010).

24. Z. Lu et al., "An Evaluation of the Vitamin $D^3$ Content in Fish: Is the Vitamin D Content Adequate to Satisfy the Dietary Requirements for Vitamin D?," *The Journal of Steroid Biochemistry and Molecular Biology* 103 (2007): 642–44.

25. C. Elliott, "Assessing 'Fun Foods': Nutrition Content and Analysis of Supermarket Foods Targeted at Children," *Obesity Reviews* 9 (2008): 368–77.

26. Statistics Canada, "Sodium Consumption at All Ages," The Findings, http://www.statcan.gc.ca/pub/82–003-x/2006004/article/sodium/4148995-eng.htm (accessed September 18, 2010).

27. Lynn L. Moore et al., "Dairy Intake and Anthropometric Measures of Body Fat among Children and Adolescents in NHANES," *Journal of the American College of Nutrition* 27, (2008): 702–10.

28. Statistics Canada, "Overview of Canadians' Eating Habits," The Daily, http://www.statcan.gc.ca/daily-quotidien/060706/

dq060706b-eng.htm.

29. David Suzuki Foundation, "The Skinny on Salmon," Food: Is It Safe? http://www.davidsuzuki.org/ (accessed October 2, 2009).

30. David Suzuki Foundation, "Why You Shouldn't Eat Farmed Salmon," What You Can Do, http://www.davidsuzuki.org/ (accessed October 2, 2009).

31. David Suzuki Foundation, "The Skinny on Salmon," Food: Is It Safe? http://www.davidsuzuki.org/ (accessed October 2, 2009).

32. Statistics Canada, "Overview of Canadians' Eating Habits," The Daily, http://www.statcan.gc.ca/daily-quotidien/060706/dq060706b-eng.htm.

33. David Suzuki Foundation, "Food and Climate Change," What You Can Do, http://www.davidsuzuki.org/what-you-can-do/eat-for-a-healthy-planet/food-and-climate-change/ (accessed September 16, 2010).

34. Health Canada, "Do Canadian Adolescents Meet Their Nutrient Requirements through Food Intake Alone?" Food and Nutrition, http://www.hc-sc.gc.ca/fn-an/surveill/nutrition/commun/art-nutr-adol-eng.php (accessed September 16, 2010).

35. Health Canada, "Risks Associated with Sprouts," Healthy Living, http://www.hc-sc.gc.ca/hl-vs/iyh-vsv/food-aliment/sprouts-germes-eng.php (accessed September 16, 2010).

36. Maria Al Aberg et al., "Fish Intake of Swedish Male Adolescents Is a Predictor of Cognitive Performance," *Acta*

*Paediatrica,* 98 (2009): 555–60.

37. David Suzuki Foundation, "Introduction," Food: Is It Safe? http://www.davidsuzuki.org/ (accessed October 2, 2009).

38. Henning Steinfeld et al., Food and Agriculture Organization of the United Nations, "Livestock's Long Shadow, Environmental Issues and Options," ftp://ftp.fao.org/docrep/fao/010/a0701e/a0701e00.pdf (accessed February 2, 2011).

39. David Suzuki Foundation, "Food and Climate Change," What You Can Do, http://www.davidsuzuki.org/what-you-can-do/eat-for-a-healthy-planet/food-and-climate-change/ (accessed September 16, 2010).

40. Jill S. Halterman et al., "Iron Deficiency and Cognitive Achievement among School-Aged Children and Adolescents in the United States," *Pediatrics* 107 (2001): 1381–86.

41. Michelle D. Florence et al., "Diet Quality and Academic Performance," *Journal of School Health* 78 (2008): 209–15.

42. Noel T. Mueller et al., "Soft Drink and Juice Consumption and Risk of Pancreatic Cancer: The Singapore Chinese Health Study," *Cancer Epidemiology, Biomarkers & Prevention* 19 (2010): 447–55.

43. Jacobson, M. F., Center for Science in the Public Interest. "Liquid Candy: How Soft Drinks Are Harming Americans' Health, http://www.cspinet.org/new/pdf/liquid_candy_final_w_new_supplement.pdf (accessed September 16, 2004).

# Recipe Index

# Health and Nutrition Information Index

BRENDA BRADSHAW has been an elementary school teacher and is co-author of *The Baby's Table* and *The Good Food Book for Families*. An avid cook, she is a mother of two.

DR. CHERYL MUTCH is a consultant pediatrician with a keen interest in children's nutrition. The co-author of *The Good Food Book for Families,* she is the mother of two daughters.